Back Home

Also by Bill Mauldin

UP FRONT

Back Home

by Bill Mauldin

WILLIAM SLOANE ASSOCIATES

PUBLISHERS NEW YORK, N. Y.

The author wishes to thank the *Atlantic Monthly* for permission to reprint from an article, "Poppa Knows Best," which first appeared in the April, 1947, issue.

CHAPTER I

In JUNE, 1945, I PERCHED ON A COT UNDER a greasy tent at the Seventh Replacement Depot in Naples and pondered deeply on the past and future of Sidney Mauldin's son William. I could see no reason for personal complaint. The war had left me sound in limb and spirit, a number of newspapers at home had been reprinting my drawings from *Stars and Stripes,* and I was sure of a job when I got my army discharge, toward which I had 131 solid gold discharge points.

The boats were slow, and a lot of the guys in the replacement depot had been waiting for weeks to go home. Naturally they fretted a great deal, but underneath the fretting they were feeling pretty good. I fretted and felt good, too. Then the strong hand of Dame Fortune interrupted my contemplation by plucking me bodily out of the tent and depositing me on top of the world. Little Willie suddenly became what the Chamber of Commerce calls a typical American success story, an example of what can happen to a clean, industrious young man under our system of free enterprise.

"I don't remember no delays gittin' us overseas."

Fortune appeared in the person of a harried Technician Grade Five, who carried an order summoning me to the office of Colonel Scobie of Information and Education at Allied Force Headquarters. On my arrival, the good colonel informed me that I was being given an A-1 airplane priority to New York, and told me to go back to my quarters and pack my duds. He explained that wondrous things were going to happen to me upon my return to home country. Because of a rash of free publicity in several national magazines, the Pulitzer Prize, and various other strokes of great fortune, the army was going to carry me home in style and have me take part in the Infantry Day parade which was going to be held in New York early in June. I learned later that even Henry Holt and Company had been rung into the deal, and they were going to release my book *Up Front* on the same day the parade was held.

It wasn't until I landed at Casablanca and prepared to board a C-54 across the Atlantic that I learned my air priority was not only A-1 but that I was traveling as a VIP — and I started to worry. A VIP is one of the army's beloved abbreviations and stands for Very Important Personage. During the war you could be a VIP if you were a congressman or an industrialist on a junket overseas, if you were a big-time movie star, or if you had a lot of political pull. If you travel as a VIP in the army you carry the temporary rank of major general to expedite your clearance through stopovers where persons of less than VIP rank are held over for long sessions of travel-order checking and red tape.

I found I was a VIP when the clerk at the ATC desk asked me if I had my own transportation arranged to "the villa" or if I wanted an army car. "What villa?" I asked as a line of soldiers laden with barracks bags straggled past the desk on the way to the tents where transient soldiers slept while waiting for the next plane to the States. "The VIP villa," said the clerk. He explained that I was a VIP and that a villa was reserved in Casablanca for passing VIP's, who naturally couldn't be expected to sleep in pyramidal tents with the common herd.

"By the way," said the clerk, eying the stripes that were sewed crookedly to my left sleeve, "you don't look like a regular VIP. Maybe you're more interested in getting home in a hurry than VIPing. If so, I'd advise you to check out a mattress and blanket like everybody else and bed down in a tent, and we can get you on a plane sometime tonight. If you go to the villa and sleep in style you won't get out until late tomorrow."

This required some thought on my part. It isn't every day that a Model T sergeant gets a quick promotion to major general, and it would have been a hell of a lot of fun to have breakfast in bed, and maybe get assigned an orderly who actually outranked me. But, as I said, this VIP business worried me. If the army was going to treat me like such a prize package, maybe it was going to be reluctant to turn the package loose. Despite my high number of discharge points and my five years in stir, all the army had to do was shift my classification papers around to something "essential," and I would wait an awful long time for a discharge. As far as I was concerned, they could have done without the whole VIP business and left me in Naples to catch a slow, safe ship like everybody else, with a separation center waiting at the other end.

So rather than take advantage of the villa, I decided to make myself inconspicuous and get the hell out of there on the earliest possible plane. I did, and all the way across on the C-54 I felt better. If anybody knew I was a VIP he didn't let on about it. Two brigadiers on the plane demanded all the attention of the crew, although my two imaginary stars outshone their single real one.

4

"My companion and I find these transatlantic flights very tedious. . . ."

On the trip I played hearts and stud poker with three nice gents from the battered 34th Division, and for a while the four of us toyed with the idea of making the most of my rank and revolutionizing the army by having all officers above the rank of major sit on the floor all the way across the Atlantic, giving the best seats to the lowest ranking characters. However, the 34th Division guys were as anxious as I to get discharged, and they didn't crave to do anything at that late date that would call attention to themselves. The war with Japan was still on, and the prospect of being sent to an atoll was not nice to think about. Once during the trip, when we stopped at the Azores, I moved to a vacant seat next to a full colonel whose window afforded a fine view of the island as we landed, and cheerfully passed the time of day with him as I sat down. He recoiled as if he had been contaminated, and for a minute I was tempted to discipline the upstart. I was like a small boy with a loaded gun, and it is a good thing the army took that VIP thing away from me soon after I landed or I might have hurt somebody.

My revolution never came off, but five years as an enlisted man were made up to me in five minutes when we landed at La Guardia Field in New York. It was raining lightly, and the plane stopped several hundred yards from the hangar. The soldiers on the plane all had jackets of different types, but the six or seven ranking officers aboard were dressed in their Sunday best, ribbons and all. When an army sedan with a WAC chauffeur pulled up and a captain got out of the back seat and stepped into the plane, all the assorted brass aboard started moving toward him. He looked over their heads and called my name, enunciating the title "Sergeant" very clearly. The 34th characters were grinning all over their faces as I ambled out of the plane behind the captain and climbed into the back seat of the car. The malicious side of my nature was fairly hugging itself in joy.

The captain told me his job consisted of meeting VIP's

and squiring them around in a staff car, and he confided that the only pleasure he ever got out of the job was when something like this happened. During that period a lot of Medal-of-Honor winners were coming home with VIP rank, and he told me I wasn't the first enlisted man to ride away from the plane in a staff car, leaving an assort-

"His Uncle Willie must be home. He called me a damn brass hat."

ment of gaping brassies behind. All in all, it was a very satisfying experience, and I would be hypocritical as hell to deny it.

Aside from my brief conversation with the captain en route to the hangars, the first words I heard on Ameri-

"Poor fellers. They ain't heard about th' cigarette shortage. . . ."

can soil were from an Air Force ground crewman to another ground crewman who was lounging near the desk where my stuff went through a customs inspection: "Maybe now they'll quit rationing cigarettes, with all these birds coming back from Europe."

If I ever have grandchildren and am asked to tell them

stories, I am going to brag about one thing above all others. Once I had a press conference. Just like Harry Truman. It was waiting for me in Manhattan after I arrived at La Guardia Field, and Army Ground Forces Public Relations had arranged it. AGFPR was a fairly new thing in the army's alphabet soup; I suspect it was tardily started as an answer to the Army Air Forces public relations setup, which was a widespread organization containing thousands of colonels, majors, captains, lieutenants, warrant officers, sergeants, and corporals, whose sole job seemed to be to insist right up to the end of the war that the ground forces operated as support for the air forces, instead of vice versa.

When General Vinegar Joe Stilwell took command of the army's ground forces, he encouraged the idea of some public relations in favor of the lowly paddlefoot, who loved Stilwell and was loved by Stilwell; hence the big Infantry Day celebration. Jack Kahn, a *New Yorker* writer who was a warrant officer in AGFPR, told me it was Stilwell who had ordered me home in such fancy style. A major in Kahn's outfit took me aside and told me what I must and must not say to the reporters who were waiting for me. "Lay off the subject of food," he said. "We don't consider it a good subject, public-relations-wise. If they press you, say you had no complaint about the food overseas." Ordinarily I would have rebelled at having to tell this black lie. On *Stars and Stripes* we had eaten like kings, because we had a smart mess sergeant who knew his way around in the big ration dumps that were usually near by because *Stars and Stripes* was always set up in base areas. But I had grown up in a field division and while on *Stars and Stripes* had spent enough time kicking

9

around field outfits to realize that the farther forward a feller traveled the slacker his gut became.

However, I must admit I was anxious to please the army at this point, and I think I would have sworn to having had a steady diet of ice cream and steak if it would have helped my prospects of getting a discharge. The major also cautioned me on complaining about equipment, morale, discipline, and clothing — in short, he told me to tell the truth in reply to any question I might be asked about the army, but to remember that the truth about the army was that the army was a nice place to be.

Then the major went in with me to meet the reporters, and he hovered near by to help tell the truth in case I should forget.

Everybody asked a lot of questions, and I answered most of them, glancing from time to time at my mentor, who gave me encouraging and approving nods. I don't remember many questions or answers, except one about whether I intended to go to the Pacific where the war was still on. I started to open my yap wide and give that question the kind of answer it deserved, but I felt the major's eyes on me and I thought of that discharge and the gray suit with the red tie and green socks, and made the following lightning analysis of the situation: If I tell them what they can do with the war in the Pacific, they might decide to *show* me what they can do with it. While if I say I'm willing to go, maybe, but feel like I ought to enjoy life in these United States for a little while first, why then I will have made the proper and patriotic answer, and they will leave me alone. So I gave the right answer. It was a very fine press conference.

It turned out that I needn't have worried so much

"He thinks the food over there was swell. He's glad to be home, but he misses the thrill and excitement of battle. You may quote him."

about incurring the displeasure of the AGFPR people. The day after I arrived, General Stilwell was suddenly put in command of the 10th Army at Okinawa, and when he departed the Infantry Day celebration sort of fell apart. They still had a parade, but most of the other ceremonies were put aside, and whatever part I was supposed to have played was also sidetracked. Jack Kahn pulled me into a corner and suggested that I pick up my barracks bag and hustle out to the Fort Dix separation center, in view of the fact that I had all my records with me, a lot of discharge points, and a nonessential classification. I think my card still had me listed as an infantry rifleman, although it had been a long time since I had worked at that trade.

Kahn said I would be wise to pass through Fort Dix as quietly as possible, because he shared my suspicion that after loading a guy with VIP tickets and press conferences, the army might decide to keep him around as a pet or something. Therefore, we agreed, it was advisable to get out before any stray colonel in public relations at Washington knew I was doing it.

Since that time I have considered Kahn a prince among men, and I read faithfully everything he writes in the *New Yorker*, even when I have a headache.

Kahn had even smoothed the way for me at Dix so that I was accepted without question, although I hadn't come in with a regular contingent of overseas veterans. During the week or so that I sweated out my discharge, only two unpleasant things happened. A clerk in the classification section, where it was decided whether or not you were essential to the remaining war effort, pointed out to me that, when enlisting in 1940, in the space where I had been told to fill out an alternate occupation I had listed artist. "Now," he said, "does the army use you as an artist? Artists are essential this week, because the army is short on sign painters in the engineer corps." I assured him that the army never used me as an artist, and confided that I had just stuck it in the record as a gag, because I thought it funny at the time. "Artist. Hah!" I said. "Hah! Look at me. I even write left-handed. Did you ever hear of a left-handed artist?" He allowed as how he hadn't, cautioned me about filling out

"Essential to th' war effort, Willie. They held up my discharge until th' latrine in Barrack 27 is clean."

government records with funny stuff, and banged my papers with the beautiful stamp that said I was non-essential.

The other unhappy event was a visit by a *PM* reporter, who came to the door as I basked under a 40-watt bulb in a barrack, messing up my face with a Hershey bar and reading a pile of *Amazing Stories*. I went out to meet him, and he said he wanted to do one of those profile things which *PM* runs double-page in its Sunday editions. He wanted me to talk about my youth, my hopes, my dreams, my fears, and my politics. Especially my politics.

Above all things Jack Kahn had cautioned me about people calling attention to the fact that I was in the separation center by doing stories about me during that time. In fact, Jack had asked the people in the front office at Dix to help me out on that score, and I still don't know how the *PM* guy got in.

Naturally, *PM* wanted me to be leftish, or liberal, as the saying goes. A fancy fable was building up about that time that I had great influence with the boys who were coming home. I suppose all the free publicity I had been getting was responsible for that.

In many ways I was as radical as *PM* could have wished. I'm afraid some members of the army's hierarchy refused to consider me a model of safe, conservative thinking where some of their hoary traditions were concerned. Politically, I have never been qualified as a profound intellectual, but my perverse nature does lean toward the rebellious, which makes me somewhat radical in any established society. But none of this is a fit subject for conversation when a uniform is on your back, a discharge is around the corner, and a well-indoctrinated reporter from a very politically-minded paper is asking questions.

As I remember it, I did my best to avoid politics, talked volubly about my childhood and my vices, and after the gentleman had departed I prayed that nothing would come of it until I had changed into more colorful clothes.

CHAPTER II

A LOT OF FAMOUS GENERALS WERE BEGINNING to come home from Europe about that time in the middle of 1945. Big parades were staged all over the country, everybody had a lot of fun, and some of the generals succeeded in making awful monkeys of themselves. The few parades I saw were made up mostly of civilians, because while the returning soldiers didn't begrudge the big guys their moment of glory, most of the boys had seen enough generals where they had been, and were more interested in soothing their insides with smooth food and drink, after a long diet of overcooked hash and truly vile liquid refreshments.

One of the few top dogs who could count a lot of veterans in his cheering section was "Ike," who came home much later. Eisenhower will naturally figure prominently in the history books for his professional achievements, but his soldiers remember him as the guy who went around on inspection tours with a grin on his puss and his hands in his pockets. He pretty well destroyed the myth that an officer has to be a stiff-backed martinet before he can get results from that beast of burden known as the private soldier.

Nearly every soldier knew an officer or two he wanted to slug when he got out of the army. This sort of thing has probably been going on for centuries, but somehow there has always been a remarkable shortage of sluggings in any postwar period. A few surly characters with dis-

"Quit shovin', ya ol' walrus!"

charge buttons have gone out of their way to be nasty
to unfortunate individuals whose only offense has been
to wear an officer's uniform, and very occasionally a well-
deserved sock has been administered to a former officer
by one of his long-suffering subordinates, but for the most
part the angers and resentments are now recalled with a
measure of humor, or have dissolved completely.

The cartoon about Major Wilson is one I always swore
I would draw when I got out of the army. It is admittedly
malicious. Once, a long time ago, a friend who had been
in World War I told me I would be amazed at some of

17

"Major Wilson! Back in uniform, I see."

my then-current drawings about army officers if I looked at them a couple of years after getting out of the army. Like a number of other people, he thought I had a blind prejudice toward any creature that wore metal tabs on its shoulder. This has never been true.

But it is true that there were an awful lot of bad

officers in the army, and there were a lot who were **not**
bad but who were unreasonably stuffy and pigheaded.
Considering the fact that I poked fun at the officer caste
hundreds of times in drawings, I don't think I would have
been allowed to keep it up if there hadn't been two
officers who were amused for every one who got sore. A
good officer resents a bad colleague much more than a
soldier resents the bad officer, because the soldier simply
feels persecuted, while the good officer feels insulted.

There were lots of no-good soldiers in the army, too,
but a bad soldier is seldom in a position to damage anybody but himself, while a bad officer can cause a considerable amount of misery among his subordinates, so
his shortcomings are more deserving of attention than
those of the bum soldier.

But my friend's prediction came true in a way. I felt
no urge to increase my officer-sniping once I was free to
do it in the safety of civilian clothes. And I have recently
found myself grinning occasionally at recollections of
things that made me boiling mad during the war.

For a while after the war was over, there was a rash of
articles in various publications written by former officers
who were getting their own back at the enlisted men of
army publications who had ridiculed them from time to
time. The champions of the officers turned in a pretty
poor and petulant job as a whole. It would be wonderful
if a talented ex-officer could sit down and do a parody on
the subject, but I have seen nothing worthy of note. As
a rule, the theme was that the Hargroves and the George
Bakers and the Mauldins must have been pretty poor
soldiers to begin with or their officers wouldn't have done
anything to make them resentful, and what about all the

*"O'Rourke wants to be different. He's writing an army column
exposing the enlisted men...."*

soldiers who were constantly in trouble and had to be
protected by officers, and what about all the officers who
were killed? And so on and so on.

No person at all familiar with the war can forget that
the casualty rate among line officers was often higher,

in proportion to their numbers, than the rate among enlisted men. But those of us who specialized in turning out rebellious literature never intended to cast aspersions on those guys, and, so far as I know, none of them ever took offense at the things we said. Because they had to mix with their boys and eat and sleep with them, they associated themselves more with their men than with the officer clique.

In the Fort Dix separation center I ran into a newly-returned 3rd Division man whose first day back on home soil gave him a couple of experiences that seemed pretty typical of the reception many thousands of others were getting in the summer of 1945.

He told me that after he had been checked through customs and all the assorted receiving points, he took a train to Trenton, New Jersey, where he stood on a corner waiting for the bus to Fort Dix. A lady of hefty build came up to him and asked him if he had been overseas. The soldier, who was wearing the Silver Star, the Purple Heart with a cluster, the Combat Infantry Badge, and six gold bars on his sleeve to denote three years of foreign service, allowed as how he was just back from across the water.

"I can't understand it," the lady said. "All you boys coming back like this. You must have pull somewhere. My boy has been in Europe for months and months, and he writes that it may be a long time before he gets back."

He told me he was back in Trenton a few days later on a pass, and he went to a drugstore to get a package of cigarettes. He asked the man behind the cigar counter for a popular brand, whereupon the man got huffy and

*"You must know somebody in Washington.
My Junior can't come home, and he's been
gone for months."*

spoke as follows, "In case you haven't heard, young man,
there is a cigarette shortage. Also for your information,
the reason for the shortage is that all the cigarettes are in
the army. Why don't you buy cigarettes in your post
exchange and leave me alone?"

The soldier spent a smokeless day in Trenton. He
could have found cigarettes elsewhere, but he told me he
hadn't felt like going to another store and exposing himself to another sour guy, for fear he would get mad. He
didn't expect special treatment because of the ribbons on

his chest, but he had not been prepared for manifestations of an attitude we were all conscious of, even then.

The war with Japan wasn't over, but most people seemed to feel the big war was finished and the rest was just a matter of time. Everybody wanted to get back to peacetime living. But gas rationing continued, and food, liquor, and tobacco shortages still existed. The war was to blame, and because the army was part of the war, a lot of people subconsciously transferred to the army the resentment they felt toward the war.

A year earlier a number of overseas soldiers had been

"Go on . . . please tell me there's a war on."

lucky enough to return home on furlough, and when they had arrived overseas again, they had told wondrous tales of being treated like kings. They had been drowned in free drinks, had often been refused a check after finishing a big restaurant meal, and their backs were callused from slapping. Few men were foolish enough to think they could expect that sort of treatment as a regular thing, but everybody who heard the stories hoped he would be given a little of that delightful flattery upon *his* return.

Of course, a lot of people still went all out to make the welcome a warm one. There were those who felt the war in Europe had been fought for good reasons, and were proud of the guys who had fought it. And there were the families of the soldiers who had not only missed their guys a lot, but had been filled with so much tripe about how to handle the veteran that they overwhelmed the boys with attention.

But unfortunately, the group that made itself most conspicuous to those of us who went galloping out of the separation center with joy in our innards and a wad of stiff new lettuce in our mitts consisted of salesmen for everything from used cars to spotted ties, petty swindlers, and pimps — all interested in separating the lettuce from its owners. They were pretty successful.

It turned out that those of us who felt piqued, because of the attitude many civilians showed toward the returning veterans, didn't have to wait long to find out what it was like on the other side of the fence. My first weeks in civilian clothes were marked by several experiences which made me realize that the life of a 4-F in America

24

"Two used-car salesmen and three veterans' organization representatives waitin' fer you to come out."

during the war was not altogether a bed of roses.

I possess one of those mugs that is round and smooth and makes me look four or five years less than my age, which is not exactly venerable. I was twenty-three when discharged, and one of the officers at Fort Dix

"Ain't you gonna buy a war hero a drink?"

assured me I would have a hard time convincing a recruiting officer that I was old enough to enlist, should I decide to return to the army. I told him that was about the only compensation I could think of for having a beardless puss.

Due to my face, my liking for beer, and the fact that, in common with many other dischargees, I neglected to flaunt my discharge button most of the time, I found myself getting into trouble in bars. First, the bartender would refuse to serve me. After a detailed business of pulling out my driver's license and prewar social security card I would purchase myself a glass of suds. There were still a lot of uniformed soldiers and sailors around in those days, and often a group of them would be sitting near my table, discussing the agonies of military service. Many of them were freshly drafted and were going through the first flush of boisterousness that occurs when a greenhorn has finished his basic training and considers himself a veteran. He feels it his duty to accost all young men in mufti and ask them what the hell is keeping them out of uniform. He can even be unpleasant about it if accompanied by buddies.

My face classified me as a youngster about due to start his term of service in his country's armed forces, and I bumped into so many characters who asked me embarrassing questions that I had to decide on one of two courses — either put my uniform, with its seven assorted ribbons and its overseas bars, back on, and hang a framed enlargement of my discharge certificate around my neck, or stay the hell out of bars. I finally took the latter course until the uniforms thinned out a bit.

I remember picking up a hitchhiking sailor who claimed to have been at Anzio, among other places, and during the drive he did nothing but pump my ear full of war stories, among them a tale of how terrible it was at Anzio when the Germans started plastering the place with V-bombs. The Germans had used every other kind of weapon while plastering Anzio, but V-bombs were unknown there. I never had a chance to tell him this, and so spare him from possible future embarrassment should he tell the story to somebody else who had been at Anzio. He kept up his prattle until we parted and left me with no doubt that, while he appreciated the ride, he thought I had a hell of a nerve wearing a sports shirt and

27

"I don't pick up civilians, bud. I'm a member of the armed forces."

driving a car while he was bleeding and dying for me under a hail of V-bombs.

I had another sailor experience while driving the same car. I had spent the day waxing the thing, then had driven to San Diego to visit my pop. He and I went to a gas station near his house to see if the two of us together had enough gas ration tickets to get me back to Los Angeles. Three young sailors were drinking cokes and lounging in the station. While not belligerent, they had their opinion of draft dodgers who owned shiny cars, and they were loud about it. One of them was a Texas boy, with the wry wit that is found among many Texans, and he was so humorous I got interested in listening to his cracks and forgot for a while that I was the butt of them. The sailors weren't really ill-natured; they were just full of beans.

But a few more such encounters in gas stations, bars, or restaurants, and I would have begun to get downright resentful toward the gents with the well-pressed uniforms and the crew-cut hair. I began to understand why a lot of civilians felt a little edgy toward uniforms at the end of the war, and some of the first anger I had felt toward civilians back at the Fort Dix separation center faded away. I realized that if I had been unacceptable to the army's medical examiners and had spent the war in America, I would have come in contact with maybe five thousand soldiers and sailors at one time and another. I figure about five per cent would have been unpleasant characters who would have twitted me a bit about my pin stripes. After the first hundred, I would have been ready to spit in somebody's eye.

CHAPTER III

ALMOST FROM THE MOMENT I CAME HOME from overseas I had to start worrying about cartoon material. The syndicate that distributed my drawings to papers in America had left me alone while I was in the army. I was a soldier, and my job was to draw for *Stars and Stripes*. The syndicate was allowed second use of the cartoons through the courtesy of *Stars and Stripes* and the army, and when they got a bad drawing or one that was too late for a deadline, there was nothing they could say about it.

But as soon as I was a civilian I found the syndicate had no compunction about reminding me that I still had a taskmaster. At first things didn't look too tough. I still had my original plan of taking my characters, Willie and Joe, out of the army with me, and putting them through the mill with the rest of the veterans. Despite my fancy trip home and my spurt of publicity, I found myself going through most of the experiences the rest of the guys did. The boys in Fort Dix had told me a lot about their experiences, I was having a few myself, and, although it was hard to find time to get my drawings out during the rush and confusion of early civilian days, at least I had plenty of ideas.

I was far more fortunate than most of the men who were starting a life that was new and strange, because I had my career and future pretty well cut out for me. Just as I had been able to draw reasonably good pictures of the soldiers in the infantry divisions because I could in a sense identify myself with them, so I felt I could be a veteran along with everybody else and carry out my plan for drawing the "new citizens."

"Seems sorta drab...."

After my discharge and before leaving New York to go to the West Coast, where I planned to live for a while, I paid a visit to Ann Watkins, the agent who had sold my book and fixed my contract with United Feature Syndicate. Ann, a vivacious lady who is one of the pioneers in the literary agency business, had balked at the idea of handling my stuff when first approached by Egbert White, my former *Stars and Stripes* boss, who had seen the way the wind was blowing and felt I would need some professional assistance as a civilian whose work was momentarily popular. "I am too old to walk the streets peddling cartoons with a portfolio under my arm," she had said, but when White assured her that her difficulty would not be in selling the things, but in saying yea and nay to the right people, she tentatively agreed.

During the visit, Ann gave me a shocking summary of what was going on in the Mauldin department. While I sat with my mouth open, she started with a list of several awards which had followed the Pulitzer Prize as a tail follows a comet. My volume of cartoons and text had become a Book-of-the-Month Club selection, which guaranteed me a nifty little fortune; my newspaper list had zoomed from seventy-five or eighty to more than a hundred and eighty; several lecture agencies wanted me to go booming around the country popping off to audiences who wouldn't care what I said but wanted to look at the child prodigy; and at least two hundred organizations including everything from political pressure groups to bird-admiring societies wanted me to become honorary this and honorary that and get my name on their letterheads.

As I rallied from this first onslaught, she dropped her

blockbuster. She told me I would have plenty of work to do when I went to the Coast, because she had sold my book to International Pictures, and had done all right by me in the transaction. Before it would all die down, I was a cinch to make at least $400,000 and maybe more. Of course it would all come in a year's time, which put me in one of those income-tax brackets that used to pop my eyes out when I read about them. Even so, I could always brag that I had made nearly half a million bucks before my twenty-fifth birthday, and when the Treasury got through with me, enough would be left to feather a nice nest.

I have grown up in a society where people spend their lives working for something like this to happen to them, and it would be silly to pretend that such news didn't dazzle me. But even while sitting in Ann's office in a chair that had suddenly turned gold, I could see the drawbacks to the whole thing. And after I had left her office and my head had stopped spinning, I knew that my plans for the future were due for a drastic change. Even a little kid knows what the celebrity treatment is in America, and I had a pretty good idea of what was coming in the next few months.

My next visit was to the office of George Carlin, who was manager of United Feature Syndicate until his death in 1946. Carlin was very kind and sympathetic as he listened to the tale of woe I poured into his ear. He had lived long enough to realize that a young feller with a sudden success and a pile of jack can have good reason for woe.

I told him how happy and surprised I had been when a number of papers at home had started reprinting my

33

"Uncle Louie sent you boys a present. Real European cognac."

drawings from the *Stars and Stripes*. I had been particularly surprised when the drawings seemed to meet with a warm reception, because I had not drawn pictures about the army in general, with an eye to pleasing everybody, but had drawn for and about the infantry divisions with which I had spent most of my time in the service. In view of the fact that a lot of the drawings had dealt with purely local situations which had significance only in combat areas and were often a source of puzzlement in places even so near the war as Paris and Rome, I had not dreamed that people back home would like the pictures. I said I had taken it as an indication that home folks were interested in the war and the individuals who fought it, and that as long as they were interested, I had planned to come home, become a veteran, and draw veteran pictures. I entertained a hope that the general interest everybody was showing in the war, and in its literary and pictorial products, would mean that for the first time in history a nation would try to make up to its soldiers for what they had sacrificed by going away to fight its battles.

Carlin said yes, he, too, was full of those magnificent thoughts, and then he brought the conversation down to earth and said there were other reasons why I should continue drawing pictures about the soldiers who had returned. He pointed out the fact that I had a terrific circulation, and that this meant considerable revenue for myself and for United Feature. He was a very wise gentleman, and he knew damn well I was going to ask him to release me from my contract until the hullabaloo died down and Mauldin was just another kid trying to get along.

Seeing that he was alerted, I asked that very thing, and explained my carefully thought-out reasons: It had been five years since I had been a civilian, and I had been barely eighteen years old when I had gone into the army. The army had effectively cut me off from civilian life during a time when most kids are completing a school education, with the result that as a civilian I found myself as much a rookie as most people do when they join the army.

I told Carlin that I didn't consider this, in itself, a terrible drawback to my work. Ordinarily, I would have been able to go through the rookie and amateur stages of citizenship, and reach maturity along with those boys who had joined early like myself. In fact, under normal circumstances, it would have added realism and authenticity to my drawings. But what, I wanted to know, about Dame Fortune and her platinum shillelagh, which had given me such a tremendous clout on the bean? How could a guy identify himself with veterans who needed housing while he could afford to pay shyster prices for real estate? How could he feel ill-used and draw strong pictures about unemployment when he had a fat bank account and no financial worries for some years to come? How could he keep himself reasonably anonymous while seeking material if such a fuss was being made over him?

Heck, said George Carlin, be objective. Be a reporter. And besides, he said, didn't the boys know who you were when you drove your jeep with the locker full of drawing equipment and hung around outfits looking for cartoon material overseas? You act as though this were a new problem to you. Don't tell me you were successful in creeping around over there without somebody knowing who you were, or what you were doing.

I explained to Carlin that one thing that distinguished the American soldier above all other things was his attitude toward little people whose names get into print. Soldiers and school kids have a healthy lack of reverence for sacred cows, due, probably, to the fact that they have nothing to gain by being nice to them. I recalled having been invited to officers' messes several times, but for the life of me I can't remember ever having received an extra portion of goulash when bucking an enlisted-men's chow line in a strange outfit. My small celebrity did not keep guys from swiping the extra gas can off my jeep or from telling me off in four-letter words if I dropped a butt in a freshly-policed area. Besides, I added, my entire army career had not been taken up with private jeeps and by-lines. While I had no reason to complain of a broken back, I had been around enough to talk shop.

Carlin insisted that if I had been able to live a comparatively free and unsoldierly life working on the army paper, while drawing realistic cartoons about soldiers whose lives were by no means so free, there was no reason I couldn't apply the same technique to my postwar stuff. In short, he didn't let me out of the contract. I was faced with two alternatives. I could draw veteran pictures with some accuracy, but they would lack a certain spark because I'd be drawing situations that I myself hadn't lived — or I could draw civilian cartoons which would often fall flat on their faces because half the time I would not know what the hell I was drawing about. In the following two years I did a great number of both kinds of cartoons.

When I wrote *Up Front,* I had some two hundred cartoons to use for illustrations, and I found 165 that I thought were suitable. For this, which is somewhat longer in text, I had almost five hundred postwar cartoons to choose from, and when picking these illustrations I have thrown out three for every one I chose. Even so, I suspect I am being rather generous with myself.

I have sat up late at night sometimes, counting my dollars and bemoaning the quirks of a fate that rewarded me so handsomely for having worked since the age of fourteen to become a cartoonist, and at the same time loused me up so with that same success that it damn near ruined my cartoons for a long time. I have comforted myself at such times by remembering a conversation in Italy with a guy named Ernie Pyle, with whom it was my honor to have a speaking acquaintance, and who suffered, on a much bigger scale, the problem that later beset me. His celebrity was at its peak at that time and although a more tolerant and generous man in his feelings toward fellow humans never existed, he had some harsh words to say on the subject. He said he was scared to death to go home and try to write his column.

"I'm going to have to get rid of my house in Albuquerque," he said, "and buy one off in the sticks where I can stay until people forget Pyle the Great and I can become a working reporter with a typewriter again. As long as you're a howling success you have to build a wall around yourself and exclude a lot of people you would love to know, because in every group of those people there is one son of a bitch who is out to get something from you."

I suspect that if Pyle had lived to come home and continue writing, he would have done a wise thing, because he knew the score. He would have seen how fast he could get rid of the pile of money that came in from his war stuff, and when he was good and broke he could have gone right on working as he used to, meeting the people he liked to meet, and doing the things he liked to do.

If I had been endowed with great amounts of courage,

farsightedness, and wisdom, I would have done exactly that. Maybe if a guy like Pyle had been around to give me moral support, I'd have done it. But lacking all those things, I sat around moping and reading the papers and trying to imagine what it must feel like to be a veteran, and I was learning to be a private citizen while meeting deadlines. The closest parallel to that I can think of is a goldfish studying in a bowl and making all his mistakes public. All that time money kept pouring in and little boys wrote letters asking me to sign things. It is very hard to be wise and brave when you're enjoying the kind of success that all the Horatio Alger books tell you is the nearest thing to immortality on this earth.

During that period, before my celebrity began to die the death of all war-made celebrity, and before taxes and lawyers and commissions and fees and a divorce ate up my roll, Ann Watkins said, "You remind me of a kid who has fallen into a cookie jar, and can't eat the cookies. You think you're rich, but you don't dare spend it until you find out whether your tax is 90 or 91 per cent. You have tremendous circulation for your cartoons but you don't know what to draw. You could sell an article to any magazine, but you don't know what to write. You are successful, but you can't relax and get used to living high, because it won't last and you don't want to let yourself in for too many disillusionments."

Hell of a way for an agent to talk.

CHAPTER IV

WHEN DOING PICTURES ABOUT WILLIE and Joe overseas, I did several showing Willie getting letters from his wife and pictures of his kid, so it was logical to portray him with a wife and kid when he became a civilian. I did a series of drawings about his domestic experiences as a veteran, starting with the one about the "little twelve-point rascal." All veterans and most nonveterans will remember how the army allowed twelve discharge points for each child a soldier had, and how fathers who had gone overseas before their children had been born, and so hadn't developed the affection for their offspring which comes with association, suddenly found themselves very devoted to the little squeakers who in many cases meant the difference between a discharge and a much longer stay in the army.

Willie had some trouble with his wife and his relatives. His mother had, of course, purchased all the literature available on how to rehabilitate the veteran. Dozens of hungry authors had seen the coming demand for this sort of trash, and many had paid off the mortgage on the

"Come to Daddy, ya wonderful little twelve-point rascal!"

old homestead by posing as authorities and writing quick-selling books on the subject.

Willie's leisure time overseas had consisted of one four-day rest period in Naples, a three-day pass to Paris, and a very few passes to small, thoroughly wrecked and de-

"How old is your problem child, Madam?"

populated towns while his division was in reserve. He had spent this leisure time catching up on weeks of lost sleep, and taking an occasional belt at a bottle of rotten cognac because there had been nothing else to do. But his wife's next-door neighbor had a husband overseas too, and he had been attached to the Peninsular Base Section where he had worked from 8:00 A.M. to 5:00 P.M., and and been able to roam around big cities in his leisure time. So his wife had received bundles of silk scarves and stockings, fine gloves, rare perfume, and other wonderful souvenirs which were obtainable for the price of a few packs of cigarettes and a can of army beef stew. Willie's wife felt hurt because Willie hadn't been shopping on Via Roma or the Champs Elysées for her, and she lost no time in telling him about it.

Mrs. Willie, who had been in college when Willie met

"Her husband spent months shopping for nice things in Europe, Willie. You never did that for me."

her, had shared with her feminine classmates a worship
of fancy uniforms during the early and glamorous stages
of the war. She had always felt a little disappointed in
Willie because he hadn't become an officer with a riding
crop and pink trousers. Many of her friends had married
officers, and she had considered herself cheated in a way,
although of course she was too devoted to her new husband to let on about it. But she *had* looked forward to
his coming home with his medals and ribbons and sleeve
decorations. It would have made up to her for his not
having been an officer. After all, anybody could be an
officer if he tried hard, but not everybody could be a war

*"I was hoping you'd wear your soldier suit,
so I could be proud of you."*

hero. So she was terribly disappointed when Willie turned up with a blue suit. Not only was she deprived of the pleasure of strutting with his medals, but she suddenly

"Honey, I've only worn it a week."

realized that she had never seen him in civvies before, and he did look a little baggy and undistinguished.

This series brought me a number of angry letters from gals who were married to soldiers. I was having some domestic difficulties of my own, some of which provided the inspiration for several drawings in the series, and when my suit for divorce hit the papers, several ladies wrote to me saying, "Aha, you sorehead. You're taking

"I gotta leave, Joe — th' little woman only gave me a two-hour pass."

out your own troubles on us." I tried to answer as many as I could, because I have always believed strongly that the people who paid the heavy price of the war were the wives who sat home and wrote letters, worried themselves sick, had their babies without the comfort of their husbands pacing the maternity ward, and spent years of loneliness and wasted prettiness.

In my replies I tried to explain that a cartoon is necessarily ridicule, not praise. If you want to say something nice, you have to put it in words. That's why I didn't draw about the multitude of gals who gave their men good reason for wanting to come back, and who were patient and understanding when their crotchety and restless mates arrived home from the wars. I preferred to make pictures about the gals who weren't basically chippies, but who hadn't understood the responsibilities and obligations they had taken on when they married in the heat and glamour of training-camp romances, and who found it impossible to sit home and go to seed while their deluded spouses tramped all over Europe under the weight of a rifle and combat pack. I sort of took it for granted that the people to whom the cartoons didn't apply would not take offense, and, despite the fact that I did receive some angry leters, I think most of the ladies reacted as I had hoped they would.

Most guys who had become poppas during their absence were awed by their heirs when they first saw them. Many soldiers, as well as girls, had not fully realized what they were getting into when they had married suddenly before leaving for overseas. A lot of young guys whose immaturity had somehow survived their war experience found themselves sobered when faced with proof that they were the heads of families. Many veterans, who had looked forward to resting and shooting pool for a year or so before facing the hard facts of life, discovered that those tiny pink kissers that smiled at them so winningly had to be kept stuffed with food. A few perennial adolescents took to their heels and deserted the penniless families they had started, but most veterans shouldered the responsibility pretty well.

"How's it feel to be a free man, Willie?"

It is worth noting that those veterans who were not wounded physically or mentally by the war, who now are perfectly able-bodied, and who can honestly claim no great sacrifice of money or career due to their wartime service, and who yet have joined one of the "gimme, gimme" veterans' organizations, and spend their waking hours wailing for free benefits from the Treasury, are for the most part single. Those who have families to support are too busy earning a living to think of a march on Washington.

Many guys who had been looking forward so long to a release from the bureaucracy and restraints of the army had forgotten that civilian life also has its bureaucrats and its drawbacks. Some boys who had owned property that had made money during the war were faced with

"I never thought they'd git me fer that rifle I lost."

several years' accumulation of taxes, and the internal revenue men can easily compete with company clerks and supply sergeants for devotion to petty detail and for irritability.

"Sam, go tell poor old Jackson he'll have to put off his wife's operation and look for other work. Our hero has come back to take his old job."

A number of employers, who had filled with overage men and draft-board rejectees the jobs left by men who had received greetings from the president, had trained their new men at the expense of considerable effort and money. They didn't take to the idea of putting the veterans back on the old jobs, especially since they would have to be retrained because their long absence had made them rusty. Although the law said they had to take the veterans back, many employers were not above using ruses to get around the law. They were patriotic fellows, all right, and they had bought their share of war bonds, but they were also businessmen who consider wastefulness a sacrilege. The trick of playing on the veteran's sympathy, as in the accompanying cartoon, was fairly widespread. Particularly if the veteran was young and single, he couldn't help feeling a pang of regret when his boss informed him that of course he could have his old position, but he felt the veteran should realize that the man who now held his job was supporting a family and had bought a house and would find it catastrophic to pack his dependents and go seeking a new job — while young men, especially war heroes, would find no trouble at all getting new jobs, and probably better-paying ones at that.

During the sudden slump that followed the closing of war factories, there was a real problem facing young ex-soldiers who hadn't held a prewar job. If they had been lucky enough to attend specialist schools in the army and were trained in mechanical work, or radio, or engineering, or any such skilled trade, they were often able to place themselves. The guys who got it in the neck, of course, were the infantrymen whose wartime training and experience didn't exactly fit them for peacetime work. I did a drawing overseas about a paddlefoot, stooped under a load consisting of a mortar tripod, grenades, rifles, trench knife, bandoleers, and other implements of destruction, who was watching a grimy engineer place logs in a muddy road. "Yer lucky," said the infantryman. "Yer learnin'

51

*"Hullo, Suzy. . . . I wondered why ya broke
off our engagement while I wuz in Sicily."*

a trade." This turned out to be rather prophetic.

I haven't done much stuff about Willie's friend Joe
since he became a veteran. As a single man he was harder
to keep a finger on. Once I showed him meeting an old
girl friend who had spent a fruitful war, and once I had
him besieged with sidewalk urchins who behave in
America very much like their counterparts in Europe.
The principal difference is that even poverty-stricken
kids in America are in rather better shape than European
children, who had been robbed of every vestige of their
innocence and naïveté by the war, and who had been

schooled, by privation and hunger, in the fine arts of
pimping, bootlegging, and armed robbery before they
had lost their first milk teeth.

During a period when veterans were big news, every
time an ex-soldier got himself in a jam the fact that he
was a vet was pointed out in the headline. An ordinary

"Via! Allez! Raus! *How th' hell* do *ya say it in English?*"

"There's a small item on page 17 about a triple ax murder. No veterans involved."

killing or assault seldom rated the front page, but if it involved a jealous veteran or a battle-fatigue case, it could be sure of a prominent play. The newspapers that did this pointed out that it was good journalism; people were interested in veterans and everybody likes to know personality angles on people who do spectacular things. But the sad fact was that such headlines gave added impetus to the rumor that always appears in every country after a war—that the returning soldiers are trained in killing and assault and are potential menaces to society. Police records show that World War II veterans committed no more and no fewer crimes in proportion to their numbers than the rest of the citizenry, and after a while most reputable newspapers stopped headlining veterans every time they got into trouble. Of course, journals that have always been noted for morbid and spectacular reporting, and that keep more of an eye on quick circulation than accuracy and fairness, still continue the odious practice of saying "CRAZED VET RUNS AMOK" when some character with a load of gin under his belt breaks a bar mirror.

During the early days after the V-J celebrations, tired warriors from the Pacific landed on the West Coast, and the first words they heard were descriptions of how several thousand young uniformed punks, who had fought the war within the continental limits of the U.S.A., had torn up several West Coast cities in celebration of V-J Day. One marine learned when he got home that during the festivities his wife had been assaulted on Market Street in San Francisco by two sailors who were fresh out of boot camp, and that when she had successfully fought them off at the cost of a new dress and several broken fingernails, they had loudly accused her of being unpatriotic for refusing her favors to "war heroes," and belted her over the head with a No Parking sign they had uprooted from the sidewalk.

The railroads and air lines, which had spent great sums of money on wartime advertising to show how they were winning the war (which wasn't too gross an exaggeration, although they did have a *little* help), were doing a magnificent job of failing the men who had assisted them in

"You boys shoulda been here V-J Day. Free drinks, pretty gals kissin' everybody, whistles blowin', windows busted. . . ."

"There's Jack O'Malley on his way home from the Pacific."

conquering the enemy.

As ships and planes deposited their loads of Pacific veterans in the western separation centers and ports, and as wartime restrictions and priorities were lifted, the railroads and air lines allowed themselves to be booked solid by travel- and vacation-hungry civilians. The result was that many thousands of soldiers, sailors, and marines spent their first Christmas on American soil in several years in barracks and tents in military encampments, because they couldn't get home and couldn't even find a hotel room.

"Car 29, mixed soldiers and poultry; car 30, frozen fruit; car 31, soldiers; car 32, mixed soldiers and farm machinery. . . ."

Many of them hopped freights, and in most cases the railroad bulls who patrolled the trains to keep off knights of the road proved themselves the soldiers' best friends by looking the other way.

I heard an outrageous story from a man who was one of the few veterans lucky enough to buy a ticket and a berth on a train in time to get home for Christmas. It was one of the crack luxury trains that crossed the country, and this soldier had not been able to get a fresh uniform when he had debarked from his ship. His uniform was complete and he had a tie, but even tough army cloth can't survive several years in the tropics without looking pretty ratty. The soldier told me that he had been refused a seat in the dining car. He said the conductor and attendants had been kind enough to provide him with sandwiches and coffee which he ate in his car, but every time he left his seat to go to the toilet they looked at him as if they thought he would be more at home riding under the car than in it.

When I did some pictures on this subject, I had a couple of outraged letters from railroad executives. One of them told me that his company and some others, as well as air lines, had made a point of reserving a high percentage of their seats for returning soldiers even after priorities had ended. It's good to know that several companies did it, but evidently the practice did not become widespread enough to provide "White Christmases" for countless soldiers sweating under the California sun.

I wish I had spent a lot of time hanging around school campuses when hundreds of thousands of veterans enrolled under the GI Bill of Rights to continue their long-interrupted educations. It was wonderful cartoon material. The people who feared that the army had created a generation of bums were in for a surprise when it turned out that veteran-students were as a rule far above their

Infantry veteran, completing high-school course, finds himself assigned to Junior ROTC unit. News Item

classmates in applying themselves to their work and in scholastic achievement. Many people who teach in schools where numbers of veterans have enrolled feel that most of them were sobered and matured considerably by their wartime experiences and army service and thus have a far greater appreciation of the values of an edu-

60

cation than their classmates who, for the most part, are still dependent upon their parents for support and spending money and haven't yet been faced with the hard facts of life. Also, a hell of a lot of the college vets were married, and marital responsibility can keep a young gent's nose to the grindstone like nothing else. Carl Rose did a *New Yorker* cartoon in this connection which is a real masterpiece. He filled a full page with a detailed drawing of a commencement exercise, with hundreds of young men in caps and gowns looking somewhat wryly at the distinguished old speaker on the platform, who says, as dozens of young wives sit on the side lines with babies swarming over them, ". . . and as you leave these tranquil, ivied walls to face the stern realities of life . . ."

Two great problems beset the veterans who went back to school: money, because the GI Bill of Rights provided them with a sum that fell pitifully short of the amount required for the barest necessities; and housing. While I didn't do many drawings about the schools themselves, I spattered a lot of ink around on the housing situation.

It will be interesting for some historian to review the great American housing famine some decades hence. He will see a real study in paradoxes. Real-estate people talk about our country's great traditions and history and record of free enterprise, yet by refusing to allow children in many of their buildings they are raising untold hell with the birth rate of their beloved country, depriving the nation of future men and women to uphold its great traditions. Broken families are often the result of forcing young couples to crowd in with their in-laws. This creates chaos, and everybody knows that chaos breeds revolu-

"Nobody here but us dogs!"

tion. The historian will probably scratch his head and conclude that real-estate people were in secret league with the communists during that phase of American history.

While some senators were making a lot of noise in Congress in 1946 about the vicious OPA, many people who were on the suffering end of the postwar housing shortage got a sardonic laugh from the news story about a certain senator's son. When OPA temporarily expired, and before rent ceilings were re-established, he cashed in on his old man's noble efforts by boosting the rent of a piece of his property, which was occupied by a veteran and his family, to a fantastic sum several hundred per cent greater than it had been.

All over the country landlords went on a temporary jag. The greatest victims were veterans and families with limited incomes. Apartments and homes in lower-income areas which had been snooted previously by people with

"If ya want character references, Mister, write to Signor Pasticelli, Venafro, Italy. We occupied his barn for seven weeks."

the money to buy more lavish lodging suddenly were in great demand, and the landlords knew that if they could get rid of their more modestly-heeled customers, they could rent their rooms at much greater prices. What better way was there than to boost the price to a ridicu-

"Haw! You shoulda seen where I spent my nights last winter!"

*"You soldiers just don't seem to understand
our problems."*

lous level which would force out the old tenants, then
drop the rent a little, but still keep it much higher than
it had been?

I have been privileged to hear many intelligent and
successful citizens argue against the evils of rent control,
and they are very convincing. They talk about supply
and demand, about free enterprise and the American
tradition. Their best argument is about how the housing
situation would be greatly relieved if all rent controls
were lifted so that people could invest in real estate and
build new units with some assurance that their invest-

ment would make a profit — an assurance and incentive that are lacking while the lid is on. They admit that the unscrupulous element among the landlord clique would take advantage of the situation for a while, but they say in a few years everything would level off and landlords would come begging their old tenants to return. This sounds awfully logical, but my thinking is sometimes governed more by emotion than logic, and I sometimes wonder if several thousand families, evicted because they couldn't pay a skyrocketing rent, sitting on the sidewalks with their worldly goods decomposing in the rain, waiting for a few years to pass for things to level off, form a

Saint Nick in America—huts, but no chimneys.

suitable sacrifice to lay on the altar of the great god Free Enterprise.

It would be very unfair to make a blanket condemnation of landlords and call them all unscrupulous. Many of them have a legitimate beef about the way bureaucracy has treated them, and they have as much right as anybody else to send men to Washington to join the swollen ranks of lobbyists for special interests and pour sweet somethings into our legislators' ears. Having been in the army and had my fill of pompous little men in positions of authority, and having seen a few examples of the more distasteful brand of government official, I

Saint Nick in Europe—chimneys, but no huts.

"*Don't bother Daddy. He's writing a sequel to* Grapes of Wrath."

am as anti-bureaucrat as the next guy. But it would be nice if somebody could find a solution to the housing problem short of letting the relatives of congressmen walk all over the rest of the citizenry.

The Unknown Soldier, 1946.

CHAPTER V

I'VE SPENT SOME TIME DOING DRAWINGS about the American Legion, have attended several of its meetings and conventions, and thoroughly enjoy poking fun at its leadership because I grew up with a dislike of professional veterans — possibly because my pop, who had been in the other war, had belonged to the Legion for a short time and had quit it because he didn't like its "gimme, gimme" attitude toward the rest of the citizenry. He used to tell me about it when I was little, and when the Legion had a convention in Chicago while I was going to art school in 1939, I felt pretty disgusted at the antics of its members. I couldn't see then, and I still can't see, why previous service in the army entitles a middleaged man to act like a college kid on his first drunk, to uproot hotel toilets and carry them around the streets, to ball up traffic and insult respectable citizens, and to make asinine passes at high-school girls. I have been accused of a streak of hellishness myself in some ways, but when it comes to portly men behaving like children, I find myself feeling positively stodgy.

As a rule it is not safe to generalize about soldiers, but during the war their attitude toward veterans' organizations ran pretty well to one feeling: It's better to be a Mister than a Veteran. A few thought it would be nice to have a social club to keep war-made friendships alive; a handful thought the vet should organize for

"Them discharged sojers is push-overs. Say 'Shine, Mister?' an' ya git a buck every time."

political reasons. But most guys, especially those found in areas close to the shooting war, didn't want anything in the way of clubs, uniforms, parades, or conventions—anything that would remind them of what they had been through.

Naturally, none of these men wanted to go home and find himself rooked out of a job or a decent place to live. But wasn't there the GI Bill of Rights? Loans, security, happiness. Even soldiers who had enough leisure to fret about the future felt secure.

Pickings looked slim for professional veteran-organizers, who make careers of convincing servicemen that

"It'll never be the same. Pop borrowed it for the American Legion convention."

one day or more spent in uniform entitles a man to devote the rest of his life to bragging about it and expecting special privileges because of it. This was a citizens' army and its members wanted only to become citizens again.

"Son, it was hell out there on Bikini!"

Some of the army's inmates felt so strongly about this, and had such a distaste for the veterans' organizations they had seen in the past, that they got together and formed a veterans' organization to carry out their ideas. It smacks of a vicious circle, but that's what happened. The group called itself the American Veterans Committee and adopted a motto, "Citizens first, veterans second." Using no uniforms, no brass bands, and no baby grand pianos to throw out of windows, the AVC jumped up to its neck in politics, on the theory that as a citizen the veteran should become active in affairs that affect the citizenry as a whole.

"Bottle fatigue."

*"You go ahead an' have a good time, Pop.
I'm too tired."*

Today approximately fifteen million men have been discharged from America's armed forces. The AVC claims some 100,000 of them. That's a pretty small fraction of the total: one out of 150—about the same percentage that one would have guessed would join organizations, after listening to countless army discussions on the subject. What about the rest? A few have joined the half-dozen or so other young groups which sprouted at the same time as AVC. But *two and one-half million* have joined the American Legion. The Legion's membership today is four and one-half million, including some 800,000 enthusiastic lady auxiliaries. In two years there has been a big change of heart.

Of course, the Legion's recruiting methods, recreational facilities, and advertising means are far superior to those of its junior rivals. It is easier to join an established post than to form a new one. Many young men came home to find that their Legionnaire daddies had enrolled them and paid their dues in advance. But after all these have been accounted for, we still have to dig for the reasons why most men have joined the ribald old Legion. Since the war ended, the veteran has begun to feel he needs something besides pretty words. While the young organizations are realistic in their outlook on matters vital to the veteran, they lack big machinery. The Legion has plenty of it.

And the Legion makes no bones about its hard-boiled attitude toward the relation between citizen and veteran. The Legion remembers a quarter century back when America's worship for its heroes faded with the echoes of the last shots on the battlefields. The American Legion believes the veteran should look out for his own interests, and to hell with the next guy. The AVC believes the veteran's first responsibility is that of a citizen. World War II veterans have had two years to choose, and a glance at the membership figures of the two organizations shows which choice they have taken so far. Why?

One instrument that in many ways has failed the young man back from the war is the GI Bill of Rights. Another great pain has been housing. While professing much sorrow over the roofless noggins of its young membership, the Legion's high command has been strongly against every plan the government has put forth to ease the housing shortage. The organization has followed what appears to be a more or less normal urge to grow more conservative as it grows older. An indication of this may be found in the fact that the Legion's officials condemned Senator Robert Taft as a radical because he helped write the Wagner-Ellender-Taft housing bill. The Legion joined several other groups, largely real estate, in referring to it as the "wet" bill.

The point here is that the Legion's membership had no vote in the matter. The Legion, a great champion of Americanism, operates by the caucus system. Posts elect delegates, who in turn elect higher delegates, until finally a small group sits at the top and declares Legion policies —but they are not answerable to their electors. Occasionally posts, and often individual Legionnaires, protest top-level policies, and can throw their weight around locally, but the vibrations of dissenting voices seldom extend beyond the next county. Individual members have been chucked out of posts, and posts have had their charters revoked when they have become annoying.

Here the Legion allowed its politics (the kind that calls Taft radical) to cause it to condemn a piece of legislation on principle only. If the Legion felt that its attitude toward federal housing was for the good of its membership's political future, then its paternal attitude is nice. But how much right does an organization have to be paternal toward several million members? It is hard to believe that if ballots had been distributed the membership, a noticeable portion of which is huddled on park benches and under culverts, would have voted

"I'm stayin' in. A veteran ain't got a chance."

against Taft's brain storm.

Unless his eyes are full of sand, it's hard for a young

gent not to see many faults in the old Legion. So his swing toward it must mean that he's become pretty disillusioned in the two years since he wanted to be a Mister instead of a Veteran. Political troubles and industrial strife, which had simmered while he was away, broke out in great storms after V-J Day. If the vet was prolabor, he was disillusioned by the behavior of some of labor's bosses. Or maybe he had faith in his bank and was a good conservative. It was a shock to find that the bank, which sent him Christmas cards while he was overseas, had become more interested in collateral than character, and his GI Bill of Rights loan wasn't what it

"They treated me fine, Joe—until they found out I wasn't from a department store."

was cracked up to be. Whatever form his disillusionment took, it wasn't pleasant. He wanted a surplus truck. Maybe he had some sort of moral priority, but unless he represented a big dealer and talked in terms of dozens, he was usually out of luck—unless he wanted to buy retail from a dealer.

He found himself being bombarded with the suggestion that maybe he had spent the war helping his worst enemies kill his best friends. If he praised a Russian or criticized Franco he was a red. He found that his war record and a dime would get him on a cross-town bus. Very confusing.

"Matinee, heck—we want to register for a week."

This was not a new story to the Legionnaires. They had been through it a generation before. They knew that when a man is thoroughly bewildered and angry, it's not hard to talk him into placing some of his troubles in the hands of those who promise to solve them for him. The Legion sat back and waited. The flood came.

For an organization designed to solve the veterans' problems, the Legion has a handsome setup. Even with its comparatively small membership before World War II, the Legion was the most powerful single legislative influence in America. The organization's big-time lobbyist is John Thomas Taylor. The members of the American Legion pay Taylor an annual salary of $10,000, and it's very modest, considering the fact that he makes most of the higher-priced lobby-artists in Washington look like sissies.

Included among the Legion's four and one-half million members are, according to the count at the beginning of the Eightieth Congress, 195 members of the House of Representatives, 44 U. S. Senators, 5 Cabinet members, 3 Justices of the Supreme Court, the Attorney General, and Harry Truman. Also 26 state governors and countless state legislators. But this is not what makes John Thomas Taylor an important man in Washington.

Taylor made a speech at the annual National Commanders and Adjutants Conference in Indianapolis in November, 1946. His own words show what gives Taylor the strength to make legislators bend their ears. "We're strong," said Taylor, while discussing the Eightieth Congress, which was about to begin work, "but a lot of the new [Congress] men don't know it yet. It's necessary to impress them. That's where you fellas come in." The

"Pass the grain of salt, please."

roomful of men, representing forty-eight states and the
territories, looked as if they had heard this before, but
they enjoyed listening to Taylor, who was an engaging
speaker with a long cigar for a pointer.

"Find out for me the attitude of your new congressman," said Taylor. "Don't just wire me that 'He's all right.' I want to know if he's all right where *we* are concerned. If you're not sure about him, tell me and I'll have a talk with him. If you hear from me after I see him, I expect you to put the fear of God in him. *From back home.* That's where he gets his votes.

"I'm a realist about legislation [*note:* one of the classic understatements of our time] and I know that's all he's worried about—his votes. And even if he doesn't like Washington society, his wife does. [Laughter.] After you've put the heat on a man, I always know, because he always comes to me and complains about it."

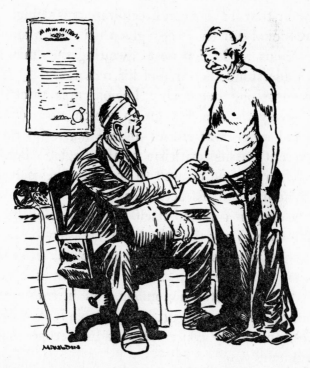

"You'll have to cut out smoking and filibustering."

Taylor repeated these sentiments several times because, he said, "the Legion is interested in 106 pieces of legislation, involving fourteen billion dollars, in 1947." This spokesman for the organization which champions, among other things, a balanced budget made a rather neat addition to his remarks: "Remember," said he, "that it's none of your damned business whether you agree with any piece of legislation we're pushing. Remember it's the Legion mandate."

When you stop to think what happens in a congressman's mind after he has taken a contrary attitude toward one of the 106 bills, and is deluged with letters, wires, and angry phone calls from his home district — and you remember that Taylor can precipitate this deluge in any Congressional district at any given hour, with more than fifteen thousand Legion posts awaiting the "mandate"— you'll understand the force of his remarks.

It's surprising how many Legionnaires think of the outfit solely as a social group which does charitable work and swaps war stories at meetings, and they bitterly resent outside criticism of the Legion. Persons in this category would do well to acquaint themselves with John Thomas and his activities.

If the Legion confined itself solely to using its power as a crowbar to pry the lid off the Treasury on behalf of the veteran at the expense of the rest of the citizenry, the situation would be simple. But the outfit is a maze of contradictions. After announcing its intention to raid the mint, the Legion professes strongly conservative politics, and every conservative wants economy in the government.

If it used its whip in Congress only to force legislation in favor of the things the veteran needs or wants, then again the situation would be simple. But in the case of housing, the organization placed its avowedly stanch belief in unlimited free enterprise above the thing so many veterans crave—immediate housing.

Practically every speech made at important Legion

"Looks like th' fleets in."

functions sounds like a mixture of National Association of Manufacturers advertising and a Hearst editorial page. Article II, Section 2, of the Legion Constitution states: "The American Legion shall be absolutely nonpolitical and shall not be used for the dissemination of partisan principles nor for the promotion of the candidacy of any persons seeking public office or preferment." Now the Legion undoubtedly has its own reasons for overlooking this part of its constitution. But the old dragon has the unmitigated brass to flay other veterans' organizations that take an interest in partisan politics.

The American Veterans Committee has been on the receiving end of a great deal of the Legion's invective. The red paintbrush has been applied generously. For a long time the domestic communists advised their friends to join the Legion and bore at its innards. But the old outfit has developed a tough shell. The top Legion leadership would remain firm if half the organization were full of carefully made holes. It must have been a shock to the Commies to find an organization as unyielding as themselves. Undemocratic

So the AVC began inheriting some of the frustrated little men with augers. Like all organizations which maintain a semblance of decadent democracy, the AVC was open to penetration. The Communist party advised eligible comrades to join AVC as well as the Legion. Smarting under the necessity, AVC is defending itself by voting against Communist members who aspire to high office—not by revoking their membership. Outthinking, outvoting, and specially outsitting the party boys has produced results, judging by the results of the last national convention.

86

Probably the Legion's defense is more effective, but one can't help wondering which method leaves its user in a better position to speak of such things as Americanism.

Some historians claim the Legion got off to a booming start because the high command in World War I supported the infant as a weapon against the growth of American left-wing movements. Once I interviewed Paul Griffith, the 1947 National Commander, and asked him if the above was true. Griffith, no mean Legion historian, neither confirmed nor denied it. He did say that the Legion has been conservative since the beginning, that its top officials have always been men "with solid, mature ideas," and that the Legion has maintained a constant hostility toward the left wing. He added that he hopes this policy will continue.

I asked if the organization intended to devote as much time to fighting the good fight against those who would destroy our way of life à la Schicklgruber as it devotes to defeating the whiskery Bolsheviks. The Ku Klux Klan was mentioned. "The Ku Klux Klan," said Griffith in his positive manner, "is dead." I thought of a little dentist in Atlanta who will be awfully hurt if he hears of this. His name is Samuel Green, and he will not like to hear that as far as the American Legion's Commander was concerned he is not a Grand Dragon but just another obscure croaker. "Of course, if it were not dead it *should* be dead," added Griffith for the record. "But it's dead."

"The communists," he said, "are our only threat." I had been privileged to hear Griffith shortly before, as he delivered a long speech at a luncheon for some Indianapolis dignitaries. The words free enterprise, Americanism,

communism, red fascism, fellow travelers, and pinks appeared at regularly spaced intervals, and it is not hard to believe that Griffith, as well as the American Legion, is fighting a noble if somewhat one-sided battle.

With the Legion's conservatism salted away for the

moment, Griffith turned to the subject of youth in the Legion. Critics who say World War II veterans have no voice in the Legion should correct their statement. The National Commander himself is a World War II veteran. Griffith served as a sergeant the first time, as

"I've been looking at young Judson's war record. It says he fought on the same side as the Russians!"

a colonel this time. John Thomas Taylor, the potentate of Capitol Hill, is a World War II veteran also. Certainly as long as Taylor is around, nobody can say World War II has no voice in the Legion.

Since practically all the top Legion brass that boasts World War II service can also boast World War I duty, the original criticism should be reworded: *youth* has no voice in the Legion. True, young veterans have taken over several posts here and there, and have even started

"Shut up, kid. You got no business discussin' serious matters."

a few of their own. But when I speak of the Legion in this piece, I refer to the Legion that does the talking—not the membership at large. The wide chairs in the assembly room at National Headquarters are still being polished by wider and more mature posteriors. One of the Legion's high dignitaries was pretty frank about this at the 1946 San Francisco Convention. "This is a billion-dollar corporation," said he. "You don't turn something like that over to a bunch of inexperienced kids."

Griffith had the same attitude, but he said it in a more diplomatic way. He thought wiser heads should prevail always, and he himself spent ten years in his own post before assuming a position of even minor responsibility.

Conceding the value of age and wisdom accrued

"In line with our policy of letting the boys who won the war speak their minds about postwar problems, I give you General O'Grady."

"You wuz quite a' upstart in yore day, too, sonny."

through experience, I asked the National Commander if he didn't feel that sometimes brash youth with its radical ideas, while admittedly needing to be checked and balanced by sages, had occasional merit. In short, wouldn't it be a good idea if the wise old Legion monster had enough young blood injected into its brain (its veins are already bubbling over with young blood) to startle it a bit—maybe jog its thinking processes?

Down came Griffith's kind and fatherly foot. He did not go along with the theory that youth is inclined to be radical. He feels that all right-thinking young men realize that poppa knows best, and that there are just as many old crackpots as young ones. He recounted his own youthful experiences, and they were right out of Horatio Alger. He jerked himself upward by his bootstraps, and now he is a prosperous businessman, and he feels he grew up right—by listening to his elders.

Paul Griffith's statements, and the actions of the high echelon of command in the American Legion, make several facts rather obvious about the organization, particularly from a young man's standpoint. If he is interested in having a voice in his country's future during the next few crucial years, and hopes to make himself heard through the nation's largest veterans' organization, he's out of luck. The Legion's official policies come from the top. The individual member's sole contribution is the fact that he *is* a member—one more statistic to frighten a congressman. If he doesn't agree with the Legion's ideas, he is not going to change them within the next few years, because the top men have left no doubt that *they* know what is best for the veterans and the nation they live in.

If the young man is willing to come along quietly and let himself be indoctrinated, then in good time the reins will be placed in his hands. General Harry Vaughan, the president's aide, made a remark which probably reflects the attitude of some of the more tolerant senior Legionnaires. "Let the old boys have their fun," said Vaughan. "They built the Legion and it's their baby. They'll turn it over to the kids eventually." This is a touching attitude, but the sentiment is hardly in line with the Legion's campaign promises when it went after young members in a big way. "Come in and take over!" they cried, not mentioning that they meant ten years from now.

The Legion's leaders are highly conservative about domestic politics, and lean by nature toward isolationism. They were highly isolationist until 1941. Men who join the Legion add strength to those policies, and to no others.

"Just think, kid — someday you'll be old enough to take the wheel."

CHAPTER VI

Despite its many good deeds and intentions, the Legion is a political machine in the hands of comparatively few. The merits of a liberal policy or a conservative one are beside the point; the fact is that the Legion has maintained one extreme policy without wavering since its birth, and there is no doubt that a constantly extreme party line at the top of a large organization often works to the detriment of the membership. No extremist can be right all the time.

Of course, in view of the fact that some unwholesome characters on the real lunatic fringe of American politics are making a great play to capture the valuable commodity known as the veteran's mind, and to turn it to their own ends, the young ex-warrior could be in worse hands than those of the John Thomas Taylors. But he could be in far better ones—his own.

One great citizen of this nation who believes the veteran should determine his own future is General Omar N. Bradley, who took over the Veterans Administration after the war. Unquestionably he was one of the most popular field commanders of the war. His interest in his boys has always extended beyond their battlefield usefulness. That's what set him apart from so many of his

"Hop in, kid. I'll take ya any place ya wanna go."

contemporary commanders and it explains his wartime popularity.

Bradley has made his feeling about the citizen-veteran quite plain: "He can think of himself primarily as a citizen and he can employ his veterans' benefits for his own best interests and those of the nation. Or he can think of himself primarily as a veteran and . . . employ his numerical strength for special privilege at the expense of the nation."

Of professional veterans Bradley says, "Anyone, whether he be the spokesman of veterans or any other group of American citizens, is morally guilty of betrayal when he puts special interests before the welfare of this nation."

Also, "I feel it my duty as an American citizen to remind veterans that their future lies in honest opportunity rather than special privilege. We dare not benefit one group of the American people at the expense of another."

General Bradley's views about the veteran as a citizen were not popular with the high echelons of Legion command. Griffith's predecessor as National Commander, an Illinois politician named John Stelle, opened up on the general several times with the Legion's heavy artillery. Once he used for ammunition the fact that Bradley had supported a bill designed to cut government allowances to vets—involved in the Veterans Administration's "on-the-job" training program—whose incomes exceeded an arbitrary ceiling set by the bill. Because of widely varied costs of living in areas where the program was being used, this had an adverse effect on many men who lived in more expensive parts of the country, and even caused some of them to give up the training. It was a very complex and controversial thing with good arguments on both sides.

Seeing in this controversy a chance to crack at Bradley and show the boys the Legion was out to make as much for them as possible, Stelle made it sound like a national emergency. He accused Bradley of everything from inefficiency to "breaking faith with the veterans." This controversy was the climax to several attacks Stelle had made on the general. The first had been when Bradley had refused to build a VA hospital in Decatur, Illinois— a project in which the Illinois politician Stelle had been quite interested.

While Bradley's universal popularity makes it unlikely that even top dogs in the Legion really put their hearts into this matter, nevertheless Stelle had spoken for the Legion, and the organization's bigwigs and house organs went along. Many individual posts and countless Legion members wrote Bradley to tell him that this was Stelle's show, not theirs. But the high command had spoken. The *National Legionnaire* proceeded to "prove" Bradley's inefficiency by editorials. No matter if nine out of every ten Legionnaires loved Bradley, the Legion hated him.

One of the many things for which Bradley is noted is his easygoing disposition. But like all kindly men, he burns with a blue flame when he's aroused. He went to the Legion's National Convention at San Francisco in October, 1946. He sat quietly at the speakers' table while the usual convention paunches shook before the mike and emitted the usual platitudes about the Legion's glorious destiny and the other paunches present. Bradley didn't bother wrapping himself in a flag. He was already warm enough. Said he: "There are among the ranks of the high-salaried professional veterans those who forget that the veteran has paid, and is paying, for all that he gets. . . . More dangerous than the German Army is the demagoguery that deceives the veteran today by promising him something for nothing."

Bradley made the rather startling revelation that not

once had Stelle, during his term as National Commander of the country's largest veterans' organization, come into Bradley's office to make any offers of help or co-operation. In fact, said Bradley, "My host, your National Commander, has deliberately obstructed [the VA's] efforts. He has impaired our progress by misrepresenting our objectives."

The general repeated his sentiments about veterans being primarily citizens. From the stony silence that greeted his speech, and the remarks that followed from other speakers, one would have thought the general had recommended the use of veterans for vivisection.

The American Legion is usually pretty wise about its public relations. It maintains a large staff of experts for this job. But evidently it wasn't listening to the experts in this matter, because it didn't expect the repercussions that followed the "Battle of Bradley" in San Francisco. Newspapers and public figures representing every shade of American politics and opinion (including many who had been stanch Legion supporters) wrote editorials and made statements giving Bradley their unanimous endorsement. Former soldiers who knew at firsthand of Bradley's decency and integrity, as well as people who knew about him only through Ernie Pyle's columns, wrote bushels of mail telling the general they were all for him. In many cases his supporters were vague about the details of the controversy, but if the general was having troubles they wanted him to know they loved him.

So the American Legion officially started loving him too. Paul Griffith posed with Bradley for news photos. Below one of the photos was a joint statement of love and future co-operation which sounded as if the two were off to Niagara for a honeymoon. Because Bradley was still impartial and willing to play ball with any organization that would help in his work, it's certain that he was quite sincere in posing for the pictures and writing the statement.

But he still believed the veteran was primarily a citizen, and it is obvious that the Legion hadn't changed any of its views, so there must have been special reasons for this new-found harmony. One of the reasons, of course, is that Bradley was too popular for the Legion to attack him openly. But the main reason was that Bradley would not be in the Veterans Administration indefinitely. The Legion could see no point in burning its fingers again by fighting him, when all it had to do was wait for him to leave, and concentrate on his successor.

The American Legion had a good friend in General Frank Hines, who preceded Bradley. In view of the loud noises the organization made when Bradley committed one small act which may be construed as an error, it seems strange that the Legion never had a bad word for Hines during the many years he ran the Administration, when it made some of Washington's most notorious bureaus look like well-oiled precision machinery in comparison. An official history of the Legion, written recently by Richard Jones, a former Legion public-relations man, even defends and praises the handling of the VA under Hines.

Many executive jobs in the Administration were held by duds who had long records of chronic incompetence, but who happened to belong to the Legion. The hospital system under Hines was scandalous. Physicians and nurses found themselves spending valuable time filling out forms and disentangling themselves from red tape,

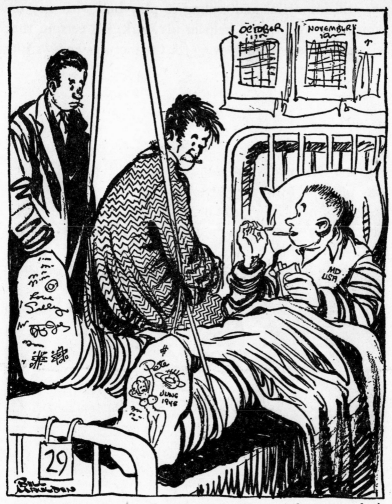

"How's things outside, boys? Am I still a war hero or a drain on th' taxpayer?"

when they should have been taking care of patients.

A complaining letter from a VA doctor, which was released by the American Veterans Committee in 1945, before Bradley became VA head, said: "Blame can be spread everywhere, but many of us feel that the veterans'

"We ain't no lost generation. We just been mislaid."

service organizations are largely at fault. . . . I have often heard the veterans' organizations clamor for more monetary benefits and I have seen them maneuver for special privilege, but I never saw them exert themselves to raise the VA's standards of medical treatment. How come? . . . The organizations are constantly appealing cases for

*"I'll never forget how my old man used to laugh after he
sold this swamp to th' Veterans Administration."*

higher ratings and trying to force into the hospital their
members and prospects. . . . They have most use for
docile physicians and executives. Such men have been
rewarded with leading positions. . . . Many good men
have resigned in disgust."

No doubt Hines inherited many of his troubles from

his predecessor, a man who went to Leavenworth for his practices in the VA. Probably the worst that can be said about Hines is that he was one of the docile people referred to in the indignant doctor's letter. Hospitals were built with other considerations in mind besides convenience for the staff and comfort for the patients.

Another physician, a man of prominence, said, "The Veterans Administration hospitals are in the backwaters of American medicine, where doctors stagnate and where patients who deserve the best must often be satisfied with second-rate treatment." Men stayed in VA hospitals for years, in some cases, without real effort being made to cure them. Applications for disability compensations piled up unopened in VA offices, while crippled veterans had to suffer if they had no funds of their own.

As the nation's largest society of veterans, and one with immense influence in the government, the Legion made little effort to agitate for improvement in these conditions. Instead, the organization often exploited the situation for its own benefit. This is one of the blackest indictments against the American Legion.

Omar Bradley was asked to take the job of VA boss at the end of World War II because it was obvious that one hell of a mess would result if millions of new veterans returned and added *their* problems to those still unsolved by the VA. The conscientious Bradley agreed, but asked to be relieved of the job in a year or two. He felt that if he could make any progress in streamlining the VA, it would be far enough along by that time so that a successor could take over and continue the improvement. Not only did he feel that his profession was soldiering, but he undoubtedly had an aversion to wading through political slop and dodging floating pork barrels all the rest of his life.

The job proved far more complex than Bradley's former task as a commander of the ground forces which

"Sorry you're just passing through, Senator. The boys wanted to ask some questions."

cleaned up Europe. And there are still many things that don't function perfectly in an organization that receives hundreds of thousands of fresh problems every week. But with many times the troubles of the Legion-approved Hines, Bradley has made the VA operate with many times its former efficiency. His first major improvements affected the hospitals. There the men who truly suffered great loss, and to whom the nation owes a tremendous debt, found that the average hospitalization time per patient had been cut from 42 to 20 days within the first year of Bradley's administration. The general asked deans of seventy-seven leading medical colleges to co-operate with him in working out a system whereby young doctors are used as resident physicians by the VA while completing three years of specialist training. This and several other schemes are going a long way to improve and increase hospital staffs and cut down the number of sick guys who, in the past, languished in wards for long periods without much being done for them. Bradley has refused to knuckle under to high-pressure artists who think of veterans' hospitals as community assets rather than establishments to cure unlucky warriors.

The brain-boys in the Legion have been reasonably successful in implying that the fight with Bradley was a clash of personalities between Stelle and the general. Stelle's behavior makes it easy to hang the rap on him alone. But it is impossible for the Legion to unprint articles and editorials that appeared in official house organs when the "mandate" said Omar oughta be spanked. And it is difficult to gloss over the fact that the powerful Legion organization not only refused to help Bradley clean up the VA, but actually impeded and insulted him.

The reason was simply that Bradley believed the VA should operate independently of groups that have axes to grind and prestige to keep up. He was willing to work with them but not for them, and he preferred to fill his organization with efficient men, not pad it with favorite characters. The Legion didn't exactly approve of Hines's omissions—it was simply ready to forgive him under certain conditions. The organization didn't dislike Bradley for his worthy efforts; it just put other interests above the welfare of the Veterans Administration.

Legion brass hats could afford to wait a little while until Bradley left. If the job, which is filled by presidential appointment, is given to a Legion-sponsored man (and it would be naïve to think the organization isn't working overtime to influence the appointment), then the Legion can use the VA to its own advantage in far greater measure than before.

Rival organizations that have incurred Legion enmity for any reason, including partisan politics, would quickly expire if the VA chose to cease its policy of extending recognition and co-operation to all veterans' groups on a fair basis. This would give the Legion a monopoly in veterans' affairs. It would absorb a large part of the membership of extinct groups, thereby adding considerably to its strength. But these would be small potatoes compared with the members the Legion could draw simply by dropping the hint that since it has strong influence in the VA, any man who depends upon that agency for benefits would do well to join the "club."

The club has made its position on the veteran versus the citizen quite plain. It regards the veteran as a separate and privileged part of society, regardless of the extent of his contribution to the war effort. The club has already attained a size and power that have a direct influence on our national affairs, and it is imperative for every American, veteran or otherwise, to look it over and decide what he thinks of it.

It is not important for the citizen to decide whether he approves or dislikes the American Legion's policies regarding everything from the atomic bomb to which textbooks shall be studied in our schools. It is important for him to acquaint himself with the fact that the policies of a group containing nearly five million members are made at the top and not by the votes of its individual members. The men who sit in its national headquarters are no longer representative of its membership, and their power grows with every recruit.

Perhaps also it would be good if the nonveteran citizen in America would reflect on the reasons why millions of men who just wanted to be Misters are joining an organization that speaks for them without asking them what they'd like to say. It is quite a commentary on the disillusionment and apathy that has seized so many men in such a short time.

Those who would make us a generation of professional veterans are not altogether villainous characters. The American Legion once had some stars in its eyes, too. One of its very first resolutions in its infancy was directed against the idea of a bonus, on the theory that what is taken out of the Treasury must be put back in taxes. Many of its old members came home wanting to be Misters, too. Their reconversion made them into cynics,

"*Who said my medals wouldn't buy me a
cuppa coffee?*"

and now they believe it is necessary for the veteran to
protect himself against society. That is their sales talk
for new memberships. But in the process of growing
older, they have even forgotten to carry out that idea
in many ways. The old Legion's selfish interests caused
it to condone an inefficient Veterans Administration. Its
current motto might well be, "Policy first, veterans second, citizens third."

The American Legion is in a large sense the product
of America's behavior toward its erstwhile heroes. If the
nonveteran citizens do not exert a little more effort to

"Yer lucky it's cloth. Mine was paper an' it wore out."

help ex-servicemen, and bear in mind that help does not mean charity and simple cash handouts, but constructive aid so that the veteran can regain his place in the society he was forced to leave, then the citizen must expect the consequences. There is a tendency among civilians to judge both service- and ex-servicemen by the chiselers, whiners, and goldbricks who are bound to show up in any group of people. And there is a similar trend among veterans to judge all nonveterans by the landlord who chisels, the grocer who cheats, and the woman who didn't wait.

110

The gap between citizen and veteran has widened in many ways. Nobody can afford to ignore men like Bradley who have given simple and clear warnings of the danger in the situation. Demagogues have winning ways, especially with the man who has no one else to whom he can turn in his troubles.

"Haven't ya tried gittin' one of them veterans' loans, Pete?"

CHAPTER VII

ONE OF THE MOST FASCINATING AND COMPLETELY useless experiences in my life was my short career in the movie industry. When Ann Watkins, in collaboration with her Beverly Hills colleague Bert Allenberg, sold my book *Up Front* to International Pictures, they knew what I thought of the Hollywood way of portraying the war, and they fixed it so I could help work on the picture. Not a single one of the successful war movies had even approached accuracy. I suppose the fact that they were produced while the war was on had a lot to do with this.

The War Department's bureau of public relations seems always to have had a very low estimation of the mentality of the American public, and since war-movie producers had to depend upon the War Department for the loan of tanks, guns, and other kinds of equipment, often including real soldiers, the army's public relations officers naturally had a lot to do with the contents of the movies. Perhaps the picture *The Story of GI Joe* has shown more real stuff than any other, simply because the producer borrowed a hell of a lot of film that had actually been shot during the war by Army Pictorial Service's soldier-photographers, who often got shot up themselves by real enemy metal. The great San Pietro sequence, which was not a Hollywood product but was filmed under fire at San Pietro, Italy, was dubbed in almost in its entirety. But *GI Joe* as a whole was terrible because there was such a glaring difference between the scenes borrowed from the real war and the stuff shot in Hollywood. The producer had some excellent technical advisers in such people as Jack Foisie of *Stars and Stripes* and war correspondent Chris Cunningham, but the expert hand of the War Department was ever-present.

The War Department doesn't think people should realize that dogfaces in the field were often without raincoats when it rained. Every Hollywood-made shot that showed infantry in the rain showed said infantry togged in shiny new raincoats. The name of one of the great heroes in Ernie Pyle's book, from which the film was made, was Waskow. Perhaps because somebody wanted to make sure no customer's pet prejudices would be offended, the late Captain Waskow's name was changed to the good old "100 per cent American" name of Walker. The only soldiers who showed any evidence of accents derived from foreign parentage were the jerks of the film. I don't want to go into a long critique of the picture here, but it was, I felt, an insult to Pyle, who had been killed in the Pacific before the picture was released. I felt that every war picture I had seen was an insult to the soldiers it was supposed to portray and — due to the War Department's fear that honest pictures would shock the delicate tastes of the public — an insult to the intelligence of the people at home.

"Dern tootin' it's realistic. Gimme my money back!"

I didn't give a particular damn whether the picture made from my book was a howling box-office success; I simply had a hot ambition to make it real. While my contract gave me the right to fool around with the technical end of the picture, John Lardner and his brother Ring, Jr., contracted to write the screen play. They worked out a fine script in a couple of months, and while I did practically no work on it, I was given an office on Sam Goldwyn's lot, where International held forth at that time. The rest of this passage on Hollywood has nothing to do with further developments on the movie which I had smugly determined to make the first honest war picture. The doggone thing was never made. About the time the script was finished, late in 1945, it was decided that the movie-going public had had its fill of war movies, and the project was postponed for possible filming in some future year when people get curious again about such things.

But I had an interesting time during those two or three months. I found the average movie lot surprisingly like an army post in many respects. There is a lot of rank, and everybody is conscious of it. There is a chain of command that reminds me of a wonderful cartoon by Steinberg, in which a large man uses one hand to hold the hand of an even larger man while he kisses it, while the first man's other hand is in turn held by the hand of a smaller one who kisses it while extending his other hand to an even smaller man for a kiss, and it goes on and on down through smaller and smaller men until one of the smallest men's dogs is shown being kissed by an even smaller dog. This is not a new thing by any means, nor is it restricted to armies or movie companies, but I was very aware of it in Hollywood. I liked the picture because it showed hands being kissed, a nice touch of Steinberg's gentle humor. I would have been much cruder.

At International I suddenly found myself in possession of some rank. This meant that I ate lunch in the executives' dining room, which I called the "generals' mess." The place was presided over by International's boss, Bill Goetz. I learned within a short time that Goetz is one of the best-liked big shots in the business, and there was little rank-snobbery around his place in comparison with most other companies. For example, writers and actors sat at Goetz's mess table, while on many other lots writers and actors were regarded as highly-paid puppets and they ate in a room that might compare with a colonels' and majors' mess. This in turn excluded lesser writers and actors, who might be compared to junior officers. There is no need to go further. The working crowd were enlisted men and that was that.

"Whose itsy bitsy meal ticket is 'oo?"

There is an institution in the movie business known as the steam room. As a privileged character around the lot, I was qualified to use the steam room. It is a refinement of the old American Indian cure-all which was applied for all diseases from hangnails to galloping consumption. The Indians would set up a wigwam near a cold stream, pile dirt around the base, and plug up all vents to make it as nearly airtight as possible. They scooped out dirt to make a shallow basin in the center of the wigwam's floor, and they filled the basin with water. A big fire was built near the wigwam, and large rocks were heated in the coals. When a lot of rocks were sizzling, the ailing Indian was put in the wigwam (forcibly, I presume) and the hot rocks were tossed into the basin. This created a terrific amount of steam, and in no time at all the patient was sweating copiously, coughing, and carrying on in a pitiful manner. Then he was taken from the tent and pitched into the icy stream. If he came out he was considered cured.

The brass hats' steam room at International was very fancy. They maintained a large lounge in it, with Scotch whisky available in any quantity you might wish. After partaking of the Scotch to numb your body and build your morale, you undressed and went down a few steps to the tiled box which was the steam room, passing a pool of cold water on the way. The pool was about twenty feet long and was just deep enough for swimming. Jets of steam shot around the edges of the glass door of the tiled box, looking for all the world like the ejaculations of the safety valve of a large freight locomotive wheezing on a siding. After filling your lungs with a last breath of fresh, dry air, you opened the door and groped your way through the blinding steam to one of several canvas beach chairs. Sitting in these chairs, naked as jay birds, panting happily, were outstanding examples of the cream of Hollywood society. A mirror was set up on a dressing table in one corner of the room, and after your eyes had become accustomed to the hot fog, you could usually see a man seated in front of this mirror, shaving with one hand and wiping the steam from the mirror with another. If anybody ever wants to film a hellish scene for a movie, they should conceal a camera in a dummy steam spigot in this room. It is like a lounge for all the head Imps, who are sprawled around wearing nothing but skins pink-tinged from the heat, amid billowing clouds of what could pass for smoke. After five minutes in this pressure cooker, you feel like a candle that has been in the hot sun all day.

When you are well boiled you are supposed to sail out the door on a crest of steam and plunge into the pool which must contain a large amount of Prestone anti-freeze, otherwise I don't see why a film of ice does not form on its surface. My first visit to the steam room had been prompted by the curiosity that is going to be the death of me yet. I survived the Scotch and the steam, but when I dashed out the door and across the few feet that separated the steam room from the pool, I threw on my brakes and slithered to a stop on the very edge. I stuck a toe in the water and pulled the member back as fast as I could, but not before it had turned purple. I skirted around the edge of the pool (nobody else had come out of the boiler yet, so I was alone) and made my way to the shower stall on the other side, where I pulled the curtain behind me, and turned on the hot water.

118

Even the boiling stuff that came out of the shower seemed cool to all parts of my tortured frame (except the toe, of course, which turned red again). I washed the sweat from my person, and emerged to dry myself just as a pack of head Imps swarmed out of the steam room and plunged into the pool, forcing much of the water out of it and drenching me thoroughly. After this sudden baptism, I went in and took my frigid dunking like a man. Nothing could ever hurt me again.

Amazingly, I felt wonderful when it was all over. It was like waking up after a good night's sleep. I could see why the "generals," after getting up with a possible hangover and slaving all day over a hot reel, went through this torture every day.

I made several more expeditions into the bowels of the steam room, hoping I would learn to like it, but after a while I came to the conclusion that, since I led a reasonably sober and leisurely life, I had no ailment whose cure was worth the agony of the sweatbox. I joined several other people who occasionally ventured as far as the lounge and the bottle, but no farther.

When I was given an office at International, John Beck, the general manager, led me to a building that looked like an apartment house, and gave me the keys to a layout on the first floor which was labelled "music room." There was a foyer with table, chair, and mirror. There was a secretary's room with a desk and a phone for Number One secretary, and a slightly smaller desk for Number Two secretary. There was a tiled bathroom with all sorts of fixtures, including a toilet seat made of some material that didn't get cold. There was a study with a Steinway concert grand piano. A kitchen with all kinds of modern gadgets. And a huge room with the "marster's" desk, an electric phonograph, and a variety of overstuffed furniture. The whole was luxuriously carpeted and air-conditioned. I had asked for a window. The porthole looked like a show window for a yacht-seller's establishment. The slats in the Venetian blinds were so long they could have been cut only from a Sequoia tree. All mine, for the purpose of scratching out four cartoons a week.

This was truly the lap of luxury. I hardly stuck my nose out of the place. I had no place to stay in the whole city, and I spent most of my nights as well as my days in that office. The night guards around the studio were pretty tolerant about this, although there was some sort of law about sleeping in office buildings. My quarters more nearly resembled a fancy apartment than an office, anyway.

I was getting a whale of a lot of mail about that time, and for a while one of the secretary's desks was filled by a very pretty and intelligent girl named Jan Furst, who was the sister of one of my *Stars and Stripes* friends. Jan had a wonderful talent for answering mail. Some crabby old character from Pasadena would write a nasty letter about a cartoon that had annoyed him, and I would tell Jan to write the guy and tell him to drop dead. She would write, "Dear Sir: Mr. Mauldin has asked me to inform you that he appreciates your kind letter of such and such a date, in which you were so kind as to offer a welcome criticism about such and such a cartoon," et cetera, et cetera, and probably made the guy so ashamed of himself that he wept in his beer. And when somebody wrote me a nice letter, she knew how to make her typewriter practically sit up and sob on his shoulder. I don't know how many friends she kept for me or how many enemies she reformed, but there must have been many of both.

I was so impressed with myself in that fancy office that I even took to smoking a pipe for a while. One thing leads to another. Feller sits around smoking a pipe, drawing pictures, and preparing to prove himself a genius of the drama by helping put out a classic movie, and pretty soon he starts thinking of his quarters not as a place to work but as his "diggings." Everybody who has read Terhune, who used to be my favorite author, knows that a feller who is the type to have diggings and a pipe must have himself a shaggy dog to lie at his feet and gaze at him adoringly from loyal brown eyes. This came easy to me because I have always been a mutt-lover, and have collected rare specimens of the mongrel breed as long as I can remember.

I have always disliked thoroughbreds. They usually seemed to be ailing or temperamental, and they always required a lot of fussing with. Mongrels are smarter as a rule, and far more self-sufficient. The depths to which my character had been degraded by my successes can be shown by the fact that when I finally collected a dog for my diggings it was a cocker spaniel, thoroughbred, and female at that. The little sissy cost me fifty bucks, and it will serve me right if some time in the future my fortunes sink so low that fifty dollars will mean the difference between salvation and despair, and I will reflect on that early expenditure. I could have gone to the city pound and had me ten times the dog for two dollars — but no, it must be thoroughbred.

Not only was that cocker a sissy — she was also stupid. Cockers, like wire-haired terriers, are so popular in this

121

country that they have been terribly overbred to supply the demand, and the result is that it is hard to find one with the original characteristics that made them so popular. The only asset that sad pooch had was that she was gentle. She was so gentle that even flies frightened her. She would actually cower when one buzzed her. And she refused to learn about messing up the floor, even though housebreaking dogs is one of my outstanding talents. I never spank dogs, and I never handle them roughly, but I can housebreak almost anything in a week's time. Even her habit of leaving calling cards around on International Pictures' plush carpets wouldn't have been so bad if she had done like other dogs: stop when she felt the urge, do her business in one neat operation, and then go away and leave it alone so I could come along with rags and newspapers and cleaning fluid and repair the damage. Not this cocker. She believed in distribution of all good things, and after doing a good scattering job she would walk through the results and scatter them even more. Then she would come to me and wipe her cute little paws on my trouser leg, looking adoringly at me out of her loyal brown eyes. She was so amazingly dumb that she fascinated me, but I knew this sort of business couldn't go on.

I had an acquaintance who had done well in the movie industry, and who had a big house, a huge lawn, and some nice kids. He wanted a dog for his children, and he didn't care about the dog's character so long as it was gentle. I assured him my little love was gentle as could be, and so the pooch found a nice home, amiable companionship, and a lawn with which she could do as she pleased.

But I hadn't unloaded quickly enough. I worked hard

122

on the carpet, but it was one of those colors that shows everything, and I had begun to suspect trouble when the studio's cleaning ladies stopped coming around to my place. One day I was informed that the management was sorry, but the music room would have to be used in the future for composing music, because a new picture was in the offing. I was moved to a single room in another building, which was a dilapidated frame structure that leaked in every joint. My tiny window was on the second floor, and it hung out over the busy traffic of Santa Monica Boulevard, which contained streetcars and trucks and honking cars in a never-ending stream. The bathroom was a long way down at the other end of the building, and it had no tiles or chrome — it had nothing but a rusty john with a cold seat. I had paid the price for my pipe and my shaggy dog. I was still welcome at the generals' mess and the steam room with its Scotch, but I had fallen considerably from grace.

I didn't stay in Hollywood long enough to horse around in its social life, but I did get invited to a few parties. They were a disappointment, because like everybody else who goes to movies I thought picture people led glamorous lives. I looked forward to orgies of mirror-breaking and milk-bathing at the parties, but the favorite sports seemed to be charades and political discussions. Movie people go to work very early in the morning and finish late at night, and their lives seem more cloistered, as a rule, than the lives of middle-class suburbanites.

Most of the famous characters I met have been overseas once or twice on USO tours, and the war stories they told were wonderful to hear. They brought back bags of souvenirs to prove their stories, and had big scrapbooks filled with photos in which they wore helmets and dungarees, and you could almost see the shells bursting around them as they entertained the tired warriors "at the front." Most of the guys overseas were very grateful

"Gee, Gertie—th' front! Wait'll we tell th' magazines what it's like!"

to the glamour-pusses who took the time and trouble to go over and visit them, but they would have been astounded at the way some stars who had appeared on a stage in a quiet rest area described their narrow escapes from the enemy, and the blood and gore they'd seen. It seemed to me that the big names who stayed overseas longest and did the greatest jobs were the ones who did the least bragging. Marlene Dietrich was a sweetheart, and the soldiers loved her especially because she spent nearly all her time with them and very little with brass hats. Joe E. Brown was very popular, too. There is a rumor that Brown once shot a real Jap with a carbine, and I heard from alleged eyewitnesses that ex-Congresswoman Clare Luce jerked the lanyard on a mountain howitzer in Italy, thereby inflicting some possible damage on the Germans, but outside of these two incidents there has been very little indication that the glamour people of Hollywood and New York exposed themselves to peril in the performance of their duties. Why should they? Their sudden demise would have deprived a lot of people of a lot of entertainment.

I used to be fascinated by the political discussions that would come up in gatherings of movie people. A long time after I left Hollywood, I read some news stories about how the Congressional Committee to Investigate Un-American Activities had descended on the movie colony with a flurry of publicity, interviewed four or five pretty men and ladies, and announced that Hollywood was a hotbed of villainous reds. That is typical of the Committee. Its members have no sense of humor. I think the radicals I have met in Hollywood are very fetching, and some of them are quite likable, as well as being a constant source of cartoon material. There is something wonderful about a chrome-fixture swimming pool with a copy of Marx's *Das Kapital* lying on the tiled edge, being spattered occasionally by a drop of scented water.

My acquaintance with the Hollywood-Broadway variety of penthouse revolutionary comes from having lived for a while in Hollywood and then moving to New York, where the first apartment I was able to find was perched on top of a building. Half the roof belonged to my flat, so I qualified as a sort of penthouse character myself. This

"He's from some Washington committee. He's been tipped off that the town is full of reds."

*"My dears, socialism is passé. In my circle
it went out with gin rummy."*

place was on a midtown street between Lexington and
Park Avenue, smack in the middle of New York's night-
club belt.* My nocturnal working habits — I like to start
at nine in the evening and finish at five or six in the
morning — often caused me to crave coffee and companionship in the wee hours. What better place is there for

---

*I found after moving into this place that Westbrook Pegler had an
apartment in the same building for stopover use when he traveled
between his Connecticut home and his Arizona home. A friend pointed out
that it amused him to think of Pegler foaming over his typewriter, striving
to save America's aristocracy, while several floors above him I labored over
a drawing board trying to do my small bit to sabotage his ponderous
efforts.

"I've made my pile—now I'm gonna enjoy it!"

such refreshment than a night club, especially if your name is temporarily recognizable and your book is on the best-seller list and the headwaiter lifts his velvet rope to admit you to the inner recesses? There are always celebrities in such places, and I like to meet celebrities as much as the next guy. Twice I even found a celebrity who said, "Howjadoo — I've always wanted to meet you." Such talk can be stimulating as hell. Every so often, while drinking coffee and gassing with famous people, it

128

occurred to me that I shouldn't feel like a tourist about it, but should accept such treatment as my due. Didn't I have a penthouse, hadn't I paid a whopping income tax, hadn't I sold a book to the movies, and didn't the headwaiter know my name? I think maybe I was saved from drifting into this frame of mind by the realization that the other habitués of these places had established their reputations and fortunes over a long period of time, while my burst of glory was born suddenly and would probably die suddenly.

I had had more than a speaking acquaintance with the international fracas that had just ended, and couldn't subdue a sneaking feeling of wonderment and guilt that old man Mars, who had started me in the same boat with several million other guys, had kicked most of them in the teeth, but had in the end treated me so well. I have talked with several other gents who came out of the war in better shape than when they went in, and they have told me they share that feeling. None of us has been inclined to act like a slob about it—weeping in his beer about the fortunes of war and his poor lost comrades and that sort of spectacular stuff — but we all had friends who were killed or crippled or had their lives, marriages, or careers wrecked in the past few years, and while we went ahead and enjoyed our good fortune, we did a little silent thinking to ourselves. It does throw a slight damper on your exuberance.

This, coupled with the knowledge that war-born careers have always been conspicuous for their short duration, keeps a guy from becoming too settled in his new life and inflated standard of living. It is not a sporty thing like modesty — it is simply self-preservation.

CHAPTER VIII

FOR A FEW WEEKS AFTER THEY BECAME civilians I put Willie and Joe to work in a gas station. I had some fun with this, because gas stations and garages and automobiles have fascinated me and occupied a lot of my time since I was a little kid. I grew up in the West, where cars are more than luxuries for week-end use; they have supplanted the horse and wagon and are as much a basic necessity as a house. I learned to drive at the age of eleven, and became very car-conscious in my early adolescence. In my area a kid's social standing depended not on his parents' ancestry or connections, but on the make of car they drove. My own family always had a car, but it was generally a secondhand job in the low-priced field, and it stood out neither above nor below the other cars in the community. One of my uncles, who was a mining executive in El Paso, Texas, made a good salary, and owned a big black seven-passenger Lincoln. Every summer he used to drive with his family up to the mountains where we lived, and since our house afforded a view of the road past the combination general store

"Nifty attendants' caps, ain't they, Pop? We bought 'em from a coupla Air Corps guys."

and post office, I used to watch for him on the days he came, hoping some of my acquaintances would see him roll by in that big black job and know he was a relative of mine. When the Lincoln was parked I would sit in it by the hour, wiggling the steering wheel and shifting the gears and imagining myself driving it all over the country. That was before cars were built with synchromesh gears and quiet motors. When you had a car — even a big one—in first or second gear, you knew it by the roar of the motor and the whine of the gears. I used to make all those shifting and whining and roaring noises myself when I sat in that Lincoln, and it must have sounded realistic as hell by the time I finally got 'er up to high gear, and the motor dropped down to a steady hum and I ran out of breath.

My brother is one of those natural-born mechanical geniuses, and he is a shrewd trader to boot, so he owned his first car when he was twelve and I was eleven. I was going through one of those periods where my ambition for my life's work changed every two months. I had just recovered from wanting to be a deep-sea diver, perhaps because I despaired of ever seeing an ocean, and I wanted to be a writer. I had acquired an ancient Oliver typewriter and was just getting to the point where I could knock out thirty words a minute with two fingers and a thumb, when my brother told me about a 1921 Model T Ford that had been stripped down to four tire-less wheels, a frame, a steering wheel, and an engine, and was available as an even trade for my Oliver. Seems the owner had given up his future as a racing driver and wanted to be a writer. It was my typewriter that was traded, and by all logical rights it should have been my Ford, but somehow it was my brother's within a week. I don't remember the details of our bargaining, but he must have done pretty well, because at the end I had neither typewriter nor Ford to show for my gullibility.

However, my brother did let me drive it once in a

while, and since then I have driven everything I could lay my hands on. All through my stay in the army, I used to dream of saving enough dough to buy a new car of my own when I got out. One of my first acts as a newly-prosperous civilian in Los Angeles was to go shopping for a car. Of course, a new one was out of the question, because the factories were still making tanks. But I wanted to get the next best thing—a secondhand job that was a late model and could be tuned up and polished to a fare-thee-well.

The term "highway robbery" was never used in a more literal sense than when applied to America's present-day used-car shysters, and within a few hours after I started shopping I became painfully aware of it. The OPA was supposed to be functioning in that department, but as far as cars were concerned the OPA might never have existed. I saw 1937 Pontiacs — cars that had cost around a thousand dollars when new and were now eight-year-old jalopies — priced at $1500. The familiar

"Of course, the steering wheel costs $750, but we knock off fifty bucks for ex-soldiers. . . ."

gimmick was the radio. The car was priced legally, but it had a "special" radio worth almost $1000. The prize package in the first establishment I visited was a 1942 Cadillac convertible that had cost about $2000 when new, and had nearly fifty thousand miles registered on the speedometer. It was a handsome number in gray, with white side-wall tires that still showed a little tread here and there from their second recapping job. This Cadillac had a chain attached to the ignition key, and engraved on a little tab at the end of the chain was the name of a well-known movie character. The salesman said the car was available for $5000 (more than twice its OPA price), and pointed out that among its other virtues was the fact that its new owner could brag in an offhand way that "this buggy used to belong to ——. You've heard of him, of course."

I was by no means prepared to invest five grand in rolling stock, even if the car had been worth it, but I was curious to know why the price was so high.

"Because we paid $4300 for it," said the man. I had the pleasure of meeting the former owner of the Cadillac a couple of months later at a party, and I mentioned that I had seen his car for sale. "That was a wonderful wagon," he said. "I got a lot of use out of it, and never had a lick of work done on it. If you bought it you were lucky." I told him that I had not been looking for a car that size, and that the price was silly anyway. I asked him if it was true that he had sold it to the dealer for $4300. He confirmed it. I couldn't help but note that he had quite a reputation around Hollywood as a liberal and a progressive, and that he had involved himself with a number of organizations that supported OPA.

135

"Ain't it sad, Joe? This poor feller says he paid a man fifty bucks fer a book o' gas coupons th' day before th' war ended."

It seemed that nobody who had a good used car for sale would take it to legitimate dealers (there were a pitiful few dealers who abided by the law and their consciences and were regarded as dangerous New Dealing radicals by their colleagues) when he could get double the OPA price from a shyster. The honest dealers, therefore, could offer nothing at legal prices but rattletraps. All the good cars went to the enterprising mob. So the dealers aren't basically responsible for the outrageous situation that still exists at this writing in the auto business—they merely cashed in on the petty avarice of the cars' original owners. A number of operators, who started at the war's beginning with a gas station and a couple of third-hand jalopies, now own huge, marble-floored showrooms on Broadway in New York and Sunset

"Some of the finest old names in bootlegging history . . ."

Boulevard in Los Angeles, and are already beginning to be regarded as pillars of the communities in which they have built mansions and made nice tax-exempt contributions to the local churches. The old pirates in America's early history, who swindled and profiteered their way to the top, forming dynasties that still exist, would have snorted at this new crop of tin-lizzie empire-builders, but they would have admired the methods.

The car I settled on was a 1942 De Soto, painted an attractive oyster gray. Determined as I was to own a nice buggy, I was full of all kinds of ideals about paying only OPA prices. I should have known better. The De Soto, for which I paid the correct price, was painted a pretty gray because it had formerly been a bright blue, with the word Taxi painted on each door. The dealer had cleaned the car up and had souped the motor so it would run at least a hundred miles before breaking down. Smart mechanics can do this to a car, even if it has been run a hundred thousand miles without a change of oil, as I suspected mine was. My purchase broke down after just about one hundred miles. It needed a complete motor overhaul, including a ring and valve job, a new generator, carburetor, radiator, and battery. The steering system was wrecked to the point where the wheels acted independently of the controls, the fluid-drive system was so bad the car couldn't pull a straw hat off a marble statue, the tires made tissue paper seem thick, the patches on the tubes were patched. And yet none of this made itself apparent until I had paid for the automobile and driven it away. Even the tires had been cleverly doctored with a gummy filler and black paint.

My second car, a Pontiac convertible, was a great

improvement. It had been driven only nineteen thousand miles, and everything worked, including the automatic top raiser and lowerer. This time I forgot my scruples,

"Just throw it in th' back an' climb in, lady. It wuz beginnin' to rattle anyway."

The sensational NO-BLO synthetic tire better than pre-war!

stuck my tongue in my cheek when I spoke highly of price controls, and did what everybody else did — I paid almost four hundred dollars over the ceiling price. The way I figured, a legally-priced car would need four hundred dollars' worth of parts and repairs, plus the time and trouble spent getting the job done, but if I paid the four hundred in the beginning I would be spared all the inconvenience. Everybody told me I got a wonderful bargain, and within a week after I made the purchase, I had received offers for the car ranging as high as twenty-four hundred dollars from gas station owners. This would have meant a clear profit of three hundred dollars to me. When the final accounting is made on Judgment Day,

140

I intend to point with pride to the fact that I resisted all these offers. Besides, I needed the car badly, and I love convertibles.

I drove the Pontiac nearly forty thousand miles around the country in the year and a half I owned it, making a number of stops for minor and major adjustments and repairs. Once a magazine writer took a tour around the country in an eight-cylinder car, for the purpose of writing

*"Thank heaven."**

* This was drawn in the summer of 1946, in New Mexico, my home state, where the highways shift with the winds and the only stretch of surfaced road that isn't full of holes leads from the Santa Fe-Taos highway to the governor's private home.

an exposé of the petty gyp-artists who thrive in the nation's garage business. This writer would pull loose one of the wires leading from the distributor to the spark plugs upon entering each town, and limp into a garage with the motor skipping a beat. The writer would act helpless, and very ignorant of the mysterious workings that go on under the hood of an automobile, and would ask the mechanic if he could locate the trouble and fix it while the writer ate lunch at a local restaurant. The results were amazing. Even the rankest amateur mechanic could not help noticing the loose wire at once, and obviously none of the many professionals missed it. Yet they diagnosed the trouble as everything from a faulty carburetor to a cracked cylinder head, and several mechanics insisted that the car needed a complete and expensive overhaul, although the writer had made certain it was in perfect condition before starting the trip. These characters prosper because very few people take the trouble to acquaint themselves with the basic workings of an automobile. Considering the fact that almost everybody who grows up in America spends some time behind a wheel, it is remarkable that so few know a fan belt from a head gasket.

During my travels with the Pontiac, I sometimes felt like that writer. I usually knew what the trouble was every time something missed fire in the car, but I either lacked equipment or was too lazy to do the job myself, or else the trouble was in some intricate part with which I was only vaguely familiar, and I could not trust myself to fool with it. Not only were the average repair shops lacking in the kind of courtesy that used to mark service stations before the war, but they didn't know their stuff, and the less they knew the more they charged. Possibly the worst offenders were the agencies that sold particular brands of cars and specialized in repairing the brand they sold. Automobile manufacturers snare and delude their innocent customers by advising them to take their bright new purchases to those agencies.

I took my Pontiac to several, and it always seemed to come out in worse shape than it went in. One California garage, which deals with Pontiacs exclusively, undertook to replace the kingpins in my car's steering gear. They got the kingpins in all right, but they forgot to tighten the master bolts which hold the entire front-end assembly together. One day I was poking around under the car while it was on a rack being greased, and I noticed that the two big bolts were each sticking out three inches, and the front wheels were staying in place by the grace of one thread on each bolt. The man with the grease gun swallowed his chew when he saw it, and asked me how far and how fast I had driven with the bolts that way. I had driven almost a thousand miles, often at high speeds. If the bolts had given up the ghost, as they had every right to do, while I was passing through a congested town, I would not only have sprouted wings, but would have taken several startled pedestrians with me as I climbed the sidewalk and invaded the corner drugstore.

I never knew which mechanic in the Pontiac place had come so close to committing manslaughter, so I have to assume he was negligent, which is better than developing a persecution complex and imagining that I had offended him with a cartoon. But I resented the whole thing very much, and after that I always went to little independent shops, where you might get clipped even worse, but where you could often get a good job done, too. At one of these places I had the unique experience of buying my own battery. My battery was cracked and leaking, and I asked the proprietor if he had a new one that would fit. He said he did, so I hung around while he took the battery out, then I wandered outside for a while. When I came

*"Here are the new radiator ornaments, men.
We'll have to work all night."*

back he showed me the shiny new black box he had in-
stalled, complete with new supporting bolts to replace
the ones that had rusted and corroded away. I paid the
price of a new battery, and was surprised to find a couple
of weeks later that it was dry as a bone again. Then I
noticed that the fresh black paint had scuffed away in
spots, exposing the same old crack in the same old battery.

That fellow was unscrupulous. Most sharp operators
sell you somebody else's old battery for the price of a
new one and sell him yours, so that your troubles at least
have variety.

I try to be humorous about all this sometimes, but I

can't help thinking how many people get killed every year because of careless and dishonest garages, which have become worse and worse during a period when they are getting more business than they can handle, and so

"I gotta look at my motor, Mister. If ya get tired of honkin', my wife will come back an' lean on your horn."

don't have to worry about offending the paying customers. I know several good mechanics around the country, and they feel pretty bitter about all this because they belong to a fast-disappearing class of craftsmen who take pride in the skillful things they can do with their hands. These men would no more think of doing a sloppy job on a piece of machinery than they would of kicking a pet dog. They regard an engine as a living thing, and they respect it. The unfortunate thing is that the few good ones left are so popular that they are smothered with local work, and the traveler who is just passing through is out of luck.

New York can easily qualify as the toughest city in the world for the auto owner. It is so congested with traffic that garage rates have zoomed to fantastic levels. In Manhattan, open parking lots which provide no shelter from the rugged elements charge as much as $3.50 a day, while closed garages are even more. Fenders are smashed, doors are scratched, clutches are burned, and attendants have been known to take the customers' cars for joy rides and dates. In the winter of 1946 and the spring of 1947, the New York Police Department put on a long-overdue drive to clear the cluttered streets of parked cars, and they lowered the boom mercilessly on motorists who left their cars on the street for even five minutes. This drove the cars right into the arms of the garage owners, who jacked up their prices to the point where it cost more to keep a car in the city than it did to maintain an expensive apartment. When the garages were full, the proprietors were so exuberant about their sudden prosperity that they continued to take in customers, leaving cars in the streets and even on sidewalks in front of the garages and charging full inside-parking rates. They refused to accept any responsibility for damage or theft. Yet the cops weren't bothering the garage owners.

I did the accompanying cartoon for the benefit of the New York Police Department, which seemed so alert with

"Tell you what. I'll park on the sidewalk, leave my wallet on the seat, and let you guys fight over it."

one eye and so blind in the other. Although the picture was drawn especially for the *Herald Tribune,* a number of papers in other cities reprinted it, which meant that the situation was almost as bad elsewhere.

The number of cars on the country's highways used to stay at a more or less steady level because every time a

"Sorry, we're full. Have you tried the flop-house next door?"

new one rolled off the assembly line an old one was junked. Now no car is too old to use if it has wheels and an engine. Everybody missed his benzine-burner during the war, everybody saved a little chunk of money, and as soon as new cars started coming in, the demand was terrific. Most people were disappointed as far as new cars were concerned, but if they couldn't get a new one they settled for an old one. A lot of motorists on the roads today never drove before in their lives, and it is my studied opinion that it would be just as well if a lot of them quit trying, before the old man with the long

"Coldest pavement I ever sat on."

"Check th' tires, oil, an' radiator. Wipe the windshield, water th' dog, feed th' canary, take Junior to th' washroom, an' gimme a gallon o' gas."

whiskers and the sickle removes their unsteady hands from the newly-acquired steering wheel.

An airplane pilot once told me that driving a car is a far more complex chore than flying a plane. He said that landing and taking off require a great deal of skill, but once the plane is airborne it is usually possible to relax, checking the instruments once in a while and correcting the direction and altitude. An automobile moving along a reasonably clear highway at a moderate speed needs every second of its driver's attention. Traffic driving requires that you keep a sharp eye in front, behind, and on both sides, and that you use both arms and both legs constantly to shift gears, signal, stop, and start. The pilot told me he doesn't like to drive because he feels incompetent. He thinks drivers' tests should be far more rugged than flyers' tests. Yet in most states you can get a permit to drive if you can see your nose, and hear a gun in your ear.

None of this discourages me from driving, nor does it discourage anybody else, but it takes a lot of fun out of it. The only wreck I've had in my life, after driving since the age of eleven, was caused last year by an old lady in a Ford, who made a left turn without signaling at an intersection. She turned when I was exactly thirty feet from her and coming directly toward her, and she said she hadn't even seen me. She didn't have a driver's license, but she wanted to collect damages because I had been unchivalrous enough to collide with a lady.

A small crowd gathered around the mangled metal of my car and the old lady's car. Mine was a spanking new job which I had acquired after the Pontiac got tired from its strenuous travels. The only personal injury sustained by either belligerent was a small dent in my nose, which had connected with the steering wheel with some force. But the funny thing about the crowd was that it wasn't looking for gore, as crowds around wrecks used to do. Eight mangled bodies could have been pinned under the cars and they would not have drawn a glance from the car-hungry spectators. They were looking at my new sedan, and they were wailing, "Look at it! Right outta the factory! Ain't it awful?" That painted tin should be so dear, and flesh and blood so cheap! All I got out of it was an idea for a cartoon, the proceeds of which paid for a fourth of my repair bill.

"Tsk, tsk—a '47 model—fresh from th' factory!"

CHAPTER IX

ALTHOUGH I AM NOT QUALIFIED TO SPEAK
with authority on political matters, politics and the
people who are mixed up in them interest me very
much. I have many political opinions, although few of
them are hardened to the point where I can see no sense
in the arguments of a man who opposes my views. I
suppose my attitudes placed me on the left side of American politics from the moment I was discharged from the
army. Somewhere in my early childhood and in the army
I developed a rather suspicious and rebellious attitude
toward stuffed shirts, and since it has been my experience
that more stuffed shirts are to be found in the higher
ranks of wealth and position than anywhere else, I find
myself more often in sympathy with the people who
oppose the "elite" than not. Also I have strong feelings
about racial prejudice, which is probably more widespread in this country than anywhere else in the world.
I know that opposition to racial bigotry is not confined
entirely to the left. A number of quite conservative
organizations and newspapers in America have crusaded

154

"I can't tell whether he's a war-embittered young radical or a typical, sound, 100 per cent American fighting man."

long and hard on this score, and it is also a fact that many left-wing organizations use the racial issues in America solely as a vehicle for their own interests. I have been aware as well that some labor unions and other organizations devoted to "the advancement of the workingman"

155

*"If he wasn't a champion of the common
man, I'd say he was an awful skunk."*

can boast the possession of some of the most intolerably
pompous and dictatorial little Caesars in creation. Nevertheless, all exceptions included, if you feel strongly about
bigotry and do not worship at the altar of the all-powerful
dollar, you are generally regarded as slightly radical in
American politics today.

The wife of a popular movie actor once invited me to
her house in Los Angeles to help some of her friends
divide the contents of a good bottle. While her expensive
friends sat in her expensive house drinking expensive
liquor, she sat in plain view, pecking on a typewriter

and finishing some propaganda she was doing for the PAC. It was a funny scene, but I have more respect for the lady than I do for some of her acquaintances who, now that they are successful, try to look like those Men of Distinction whisky ads, and who do their best to convey the impression that they are born aristocrats.

That lady worked at her politics, and as long as a person works at his beliefs, I can't go along with some of the wise guys who say that well-heeled radicals ought to live like workingmen if they love the workers so much. It would be equally silly to condemn a poor man for being a stanchly conservative Republican. The real parlor pink doesn't work at his "beliefs." He just spouts when he's sure he's in safe company.

I do not wish to give the impression that all major and minor figures in the Broadway-Hollywood mob whose politics are leftish are phonies. Most people who have achieved success in the film, radio, theater, or writing trades did so at the cost of years of hard work and patience, and most of them started at the bottom of the heap. There are a number who haven't forgotten the days of ten-cent lunches, who still bear the scars inflicted by springs that burst through worn mattresses in fifty-cent hotel rooms, and who realize that for every success at the top there are twenty equally talented and equally hard-working people at the bottom who haven't been blessed with the breaks. Some of them sleep better at night because their politics are on the side of the people at the bottom.

Because I was momentarily successful in a financial way, and was in a position to rub elbows with high-bracket radicals, I suppose that when I launch any kicks at their broad fannies, I must perform the rather remarkable feat of running ahead of my foot and baring my own bottom. But even at the risk of a bruised posterior, I can't resist making a few drawings and writing a few words about the champagne-bucket liberals.

Such characters sometimes remind me of a guy I knew when I grew up in the West. He was a successful farmer and one of the worst Scrooges the world ever saw. He was not above clipping his neighbors, and he specialized in dropping around when they were in financial trouble, with the result that he soon owned a lot of farms. By some standards he was a booming success as a 100 per cent American free-enterpriser, but by my standards he was a horse's tail. This rich old boy could be seen in church every Sunday, and of course he did a lot for the church. I remember him especially because he was the first grown man I ever saw cry. We had a visiting preacher who was an evangelist with a streak of Holy Roller in him, and when he would get on the subject of the evils of money (which pleased most of us because we didn't have any) this old farmer would break out in sobs. Then he would go home, presumably sniffle himself to sleep, and wake up Monday morning and foreclose another mortgage.

The phony variety of parlor pink has his Sunday between midnight and 4 A.M., at which time he bewails the plight of the common man. He does this in the presence of his friends whom he can trust, and he never lets his Sunday attitude interfere with his working days, which he begins at 2 P.M., and during which he sees how many "filthy dollars" he can pry from "dirty capitalist" and "common man" alike.

"What's a mass, Clancy?"

If you mingle with fair-weather radicals, a couple of expressions penetrate your ears with tiresome frequency. One is common man, meaning people who punch time clocks, and the other is liberal, meaning the speaker. One of the few services contributed to mankind by such pomposities as Pegler has been the constant railing they have done against the self-styled Messiahs who refer to the common man. Anyone who uses such an expression implies that the population outside of Washington, New York, and Los Angeles is an anonymous mass and that individuality is reserved for such uncommon people as himself.

"Next time we have to go to New York let's drive a car. I've always wondered what the country looked like between here and there."

Most of Webster's definitions for "liberal" have to do with generosity. The idea seems to be that if you are generous with your possessions, or with your tolerance for another's viewpoint, you are liberal. Few people I have met who have repeatedly called themselves liberal live up to those specifications. I have had some fun occasionally with cartoons in which I applied Webster's definitions to groups that called themselves by special names, but whose actions put brand-new meaning behind those names.

"*I thought you said this joint was full of liberals.*"

At that time I had a large newspaper circulation, but it was by no means invulnerable and my stuff was being sold on the merits of the war drawings I had done. There was a lifting of eyebrows among some of the editors who were using my drawings, partly because they were justifiably surprised that within a few months of my initiation into civilian life I should presume to take sides in involved domestic controversies, and partly because the stand I took on these controversies was contrary to the editorial policy of some of my papers. Cancellations began pouring in, and I started losing circulation almost as fast as I had gained it.

Actually, I did very little stuff on labor unions or the merits of the Democrat versus the Republican party. But I did tread heavily on two touchy subjects — racial bigotry and our relations with the rest of the world.

I remember that one of the first shocks I got when I went to live in California after being discharged was the attitude among many residents toward the Japanese-Americans on the West Coast. I had grown up in New Mexico and Arizona, where I had heard some talk in my childhood about the "Japs" and the "Chinks" who "worked so cheaply and threatened the standard of living of the white men," but there hadn't been much of it, because in the places where I had lived Orientals were very scarce. The prejudices I had picked up early in life were confined to a vague feeling of aloofness toward people of Mexican extraction, who account for a good part of the population in that area, and a mild anti-Semitism, which came more from hearsay than anything else. So, because my childhood had been luckily devoid of extensive indoctrination in the glories of being a white Protestant, I came out of the army minus the few prejudices I had carried into it. During my service, I had seen some boorish Negroes, some unpleasant Jews, and some obnoxious Catholics, but I couldn't honestly say that there were any more bums in their ranks than among the "pure." The behavior of the soldiers I saw was good

162

"Mommy says I gotta quit seein' ya, Butch. Ya got minorities or somethin'."

or bad in accordance with their upbringing and their character, rather than with their faith or ancestry.

It would be lovely if the statement, made by so many idealists, were true—that association with all races, creeds, and colors in the army cured everybody of his prejudices.

Men from some areas had been taught almost from birth by family, friends, teachers, and even clergymen in some cases, to hate racial or religious groups other than their own. A few years in the army will not delouse a mind that has been that thoroughly poisoned. If a drunken Negro soldier made a spectacle of himself, he was typical of all Negroes; if a Jewish soldier was brave, he proved that Jews are troublesome; if he was timid, he proved the Jews are cowards; if he had money, he proved that Jews are selfish; if he was broke, he proved that Jews are worthless. To the minds of the indoctrinated, a bad non-Aryan was typical of his group, while a bad Aryan was nothing but a single renegade. Those of us whose indoctrination had been slight were lucky, because we were able to see all kinds of people under all kinds of conditions and were able to apply logic and come out with the conclusion that there are heels and heroes in every family.

But if my other prejudices had just sort of disappeared, I became positively lyrical about the Japanese-Americans. I saw a great deal of them in Italy where they had been formed into a battalion that fought with the 34th Division, and into two full regiments that sort of free-lanced around doing heavy fighting for everybody. Some of the boys in those outfits were from the West Coast, and some from Hawaii. A great deal has been written about their prowess, and I won't go into details, except to say that, to my knowledge and the knowledge of numerous others who had the opportunity of watching a lot of different outfits overseas, no combat unit in the army could exceed them in loyalty, hard work, courage, and sacrifice. Hardly a man of them hadn't been decorated at least twice, and their casualty rates were appalling. And if a skeptic

164

wonders whether these aren't just "Japanese characteristics," he would do well to stifle the thought if he is around an infantry veteran who had experience with

"I ain't got a chance, Joe—I had too many blood transfusions overseas."

the Nisei units. Except for facial characteristics, there was nothing to identify them with the soldiers who fought for the land of Hirohito.

We all heard a lot about suicide attacks and thirty-mile marches performed, with a handful of rice, by the Imperial Japanese Army. If the Nisei in Italy didn't get fed right, they raised hell just like any other American soldier. They liked to come to town on passes and make whoopee as much as anybody else, and they certainly wanted to survive the war as much as their fellow soldiers in other units. But when they were in the line, they worked harder than anybody else because they wanted to prove something. They were willing to take extra chances and do extra jobs in hopes that a grateful nation would maybe give their families, many of whom were in concentration camps formally known as "relocation centers," a few breaks that were long overdue. A lot of us who were in Italy used to scratch our heads and wonder how we would feel if we were wearing the uniform of a country that mistreated our families. Most of us came to the conclusion that we would be pretty damn sulky about it, and we marveled at those guys who didn't sulk but took a positive attitude about it and showed more character and guts per man than any ten of the rest of us. As far as the army in Italy was concerned, the Nisei could do no wrong. We were proud to be wearing the same uniform.

The American Indians were like that, too. Several thousand had trained in my division, and had gone overseas with it. Few of them survived the war, because they were such conscientious soldiers that they got themselves killed very rapidly. Their families, too, were getting rather negligent treatment from the nation that had been theirs long before 100 per cent Americans got there. But the Indians, while they had been neglected and double-crossed for generations, didn't come home to quite the same kind of unspeakably raw deal that the Nisei got.

"Can't ya read signs?"

The Nisei came home loaded with medals and covered with scars and minus limbs and eyes, and they found themselves getting kicked out of Arizona barbershops and San Francisco restaurants just as if they had never left home. Even some prejudiced people were appalled by the sight of a one-legged soldier with a Purple Heart getting a physical knocking-around by a pot-bellied, sound-limbed merchant or doorman, so there was a flurry of public indignation, but it didn't last. William Randolph Hearst, whose papers appear all over the country, and who thrives on local prejudices (his Southern papers are anti-Negro, his Western papers are anti-Oriental, and his Eastern papers are anti-everything) had never stopped beating the drum about the Yellow Peril. Indeed he was one of those who agitated for the relocation plan, which took advantage of the war and rid the West Coast of its Japanese-American population. When the Nisei veterans and their families trickled back after the war they found that their homes, farms, and businesses had been taken over by lazy white trash whose prejudices were based largely on commercialism, and who naturally had no desire to move out. They could never have built the homes and businesses or developed the farms themselves, because that took sacrifice, thrift, and backbreaking labor. Inspired by the Hearst papers and their own self-ish motives, these usurpers found it easier to scare the Nisei away than to return the property or to pay for it.

In a commendable effort to help the situation, the War Department sent several white officers, who had served with the Nisei units in Italy and France, around the West Coast on lecture tours, so they could tell the farmers and businessmen about the job the Nisei had done

"Naw—we don't hafta worry about th' owner comin' back. He wuz killed in Italy."

in the war and appeal to their instincts for fair-mindedness. It wasn't much use. In Los Angeles I talked to a first lieutenant who had just finished one of the tours late in 1945. He had been with one of the regiments in Italy, and had seen hundreds of the Nisei boys, whom he had learned to love and respect, killed in action. He told me about paying a visit to a vegetable-packing shed in the northern part of California, where a lanky farmer asked him, "How many of them Japs in your company got killed?" "All but two of the men who started in my platoon were killed by the end of the war," the lieutenant replied. "Too goddam bad they didn't get the last two," said the farmer. This lieutenant, who evidently learned a lot about self-control in the war, told me he didn't reply, because he was working for the War Department. "I live in the East," he said, "but when I get my discharge I am going to come back out here and kick that bastard's face in." The lieutenant got a little excited as he told the story. "I would like to trade that son of a bitch," he said, "and his whole goddam family, including all his first cousins and second cousins, and maybe his third cousins, for the life of any one of those kids I knew."

I couldn't help being a little amused at the fact that the same West Coast businessmen and farmers who wailed about the Yellow Peril and the threat of hardworking, cheap labor to the prevailing standard of living are the very same people who yap about free enterprise, the values of thrift, the dangers of labor unions and their short working hours, and the glories of open markets and free competition.

During that time I discovered that if your name has any possible value as a sponsor on a political organization's letterhead, and your politics lean in the right direction (right direction, of course, depends on the purpose of the organization), it is very difficult to avoid becoming involved. Of the dozens of leftish outfits available, I joined one and found myself elected a member of the board of directors almost immediately. I don't know who elected me, but I attended one board meeting at which my opinions were neither offered nor solicited. I then resigned because the outfit, while professing no connection with extreme elements of the left, seemed always quite loud on matters that favored Russia, and strangely quiet on such then-urgent subjects as the British loan. This alone might not have caused me to quit, because it would have been interesting and educational to go to board meetings and argue about the outfit's policies. But I was out of town a good part of the time, which meant that my name would show as a director of an organization that was doing business without benefit of my vote. I was getting in enough trouble on my own without somebody else doing it for me.

I attended several banquets, and once in Los Angeles I made a speech to help raise $11,000 for a hospital in Toulouse for the benefit of Spanish Republicans who had been crippled in the war against Franco. While I was aware of the sponsorship of some of these dinners and fund-raising affairs, I approved heartily, and still do, of any efforts made for the benefit of the people who fought the first round against Hitler's boys. It is rather trite, but still valid, to say that if Franco's enemies did a bad thing by fighting him, then an awful lot of recent Allied graves all over Europe are also filled with criminals. I don't subscribe to the familiar story that everybody who fought Franco was a Commie, and if I can do something to help a bunch of battered guys who made the going a

"You have just heard our commentator read the Gettysburg Address. The opinions expressed do not necessarily reflect our sponsor's point of view."

little easier for the rest of us who followed along later in the war, I'm happy to do it.

I became acquainted with a few radio and newspaper commentators during those days, and those who were left of the center line were beginning to have rocky going. The tremendous swing toward the right which occurred in America after World War I was beginning again. Only those commentators whose popularity and daily following were tremendous were able to continue getting away with naughty sayings. Winchell, who is by no means a left-winger, but whose devotion to Roosevelt and outbursts about bigotry had placed him more or less in the radical camp, was one of the few who continued saying the same things he had always said. Most of the others either changed their opinions or were canned.

In a sense, "the men were separated from the boys," as the army saying goes. While nobody can honestly object — in a land supposed to be devoted to free speech — to the existence of a columnist whose words and opinions have always been conservative or even rabidly right wing, one can't help being a little disgusted with a man whose output was quite liberal at a time when it was safe to be that way, but who is more than willing to jump to the

other side if his circulation and his income are threatened. There were a number of champagne radicals who became strangely quiet, although recently the air around them had been blue with invective against the "reactionaries who threaten the cause of true progress," et cetera.

"*Of course he's objective. He's never been there.*"

The few who stuck, right or wrong, with their convictions, often wound up with small radio stations after being kicked off big networks, or with dwindling circulation if they were writing for a living. All this stuff led to the drawing of the rich man and the bum on the park bench. It was pretty well true that the only person who

"Let's talk honest about politics, Mister. You can afford
it, an' I got nothin' to lose by it."

could continue to talk radical talk were those who had
nothing to lose, or those who were too powerful to lose
anything.

Although I did a lot of drawings and made myself
rather noisy on the subject of racial prejudice after I

got out of the army, I didn't beat the drum too hard about the "glorious war and the ideals for which we fought," as a great number of people were doing. I did it a couple of times, but I felt positively ashamed afterward, because it was a phony attitude to take, and smelled strongly of propaganda rather than fact.

While Germany's treatment of non-Aryans in general and Jews in particular revolted and outraged the better instincts of the people in most other nations — even those who were mildly anti-Semitic but objected to carrying it to murderous extremes — nevertheless it didn't anger anybody enough to cause them to fight. The communists, who have used the racial persecution existing in nations outside Russia as a potent propaganda weapon for their own purposes, once seemed rather tolerant of Germany's pogroms. Indeed the Russians once undertook to defend the Nazi regime against its critics. Although they didn't endorse Julius Streicher's activities, they went to war for other reasons than taking up the cudgel for the underdog.

If the American army fought Germany to protect minorities from persecution, it is one of the bitterest laughs in history, because our army seldom relaxed its strict Jim Crow policies, and I have heard several soldiers wonder aloud if maybe Hitler wasn't doing humanity some good by ridding Europe of its Jews.

And the British could hardly qualify as crusaders for the rights of man. If they fought the war for shiny ideals and the salvation of the persecuted, they forgot their aims with the signing of the peace. The same people who were behind barbed wire under the Germans are still inside looking out, with British guards instead of storm troopers. In fact, the British actually used German prisoners of war to help work on detention camps in Cyprus for internees who had tried to enter Palestine against the wishes of the powers that be. While the Germans were technically prisoners, nevertheless they were on the outside driving staples in the fence posts that held the Jews inside, so the internees, most of whom were graduates of Dachau, Buchenwald, or other such places, must have felt right at home.

While many soldiers who volunteered to tangle with Adolf's butcher boys did so for idealistic reasons, none of the Allied nations as a whole wore a halo into battle.

"Them old eagles sure spoil that new uniform, Colonel."

German PW's being used as workmen during construction of detention camps in Palestine. News Item

So I stopped using that line almost as soon as I started it.

Like everybody else who raises a storm about racial problems in America, I took my share of cracks at the Negro situation in the South. But I could never learn to

"Have we met before? . . . Buchenwald . . . Dachau . . . the
Belgian Underground . . . ?"

admire the Northern liberal who stays securely in his
fortress above the Mason-Dixon line where it is generally
safe to be abusive toward Southerners, and who seems
to ignore a number of useful facts about the ancient
Yankee-Rebel feud.

He forgets first that it was the Northern businessmen

179

and the English who brought the slaves to America, under such abominable conditions that great numbers of them died in early captivity and during the journey from Africa to our fair shores. And he forgets that the South's angry and bitter fear of the Negroes is due, in large part, to the post-Civil War period, when in the first flush of freedom numbers of Negroes were elected to high legislative offices even in such states as Mississippi. The only experience that qualified them for such responsibilities was a lifetime of working as field hands and menials. The result must have been very much like the conditions that always

"I unnerstand our congressmen are worryin'
about democracy in th' Balkans."

exist after revolutions; the underdog is at last equal with his master, and his long-pent-up resentment and his intoxication with sudden power sometimes lead him to commit grave excesses. Today the penalty is still being paid by Negroes for the troubles of the reconstruction period, which were in great part stirred up by Northern opportunists who flocked to the South after its defeat. This is childishly elementary American history, but some liberals in the North seem painfully in need of some education on the subject.

I don't undertake to defend the South's behavior in regard to Negroes today, but I think people should hesitate to jump into the subject with both feet without a great deal of study of the periods before and after the Civil War — and certainly no Northerner has a right to ignore the situation in his own back yard. Physical abuse of the Negro is at a minimum in the North; but sometimes one wonders whether it is better to know how you stand, as in the South, where if a Negro tries to act like a human being he knows his teeth will be kicked in, or to undergo the agonies of psychological persecution, as in the North, where Negroes can ride in any part of a trolley but are never treated as anything but second-class citizens. It is noteworthy that much of the loud noise from Northern "liberals" about the Negro problem comes from expensive New York cafés where I can't recall ever having seen a Negro customer.

Despite all this, I'm very much in favor of intelligent agitation on the subject, because without it the gradual reforms which are the best solution will never come about. I feel strongly about abolishing the poll tax and other bars to Negro voting, not only because we are hypocritical as hell about our Republic so long as we don't, but because if Negroes can vote, politicians will cater to them. Then Negroes will get schools which will enable them to become educated and raise their standard of living to the point where they will become part of our

Democracy: *Government by the people collectively by elected representatives.*Webster's

society. Once a Negro child has a fighting chance at an education and a job like everybody else, the burden should rightfully be on him to make a man or a bum of himself. I think people who feel the urge to take Negroes by the hand and carry them upward, rather than simply provide the ladder which is their due and let them climb it themselves, are insulting the Negro and saying

"Wouldn't this here anti-poll-tax law kinda lower Elmer's social position? He's th' town voter."

by inference that he can never be more than a child.

I remember having a conversation with a Negro reporter from a Harlem newspaper, in the course of which I used the unfortunate word tolerance. "Damn it," he exploded, "I don't want to be tolerated!" So I looked up the word "tolerate" in the dictionary, and discovered that when you tolerate people you are overlooking the fact that they might be unpleasant. I got his point.

I did the drawing about the Romans because I got sick of hearing that old business, "Do ya want yer datter ta marry a nigger?" every time the Negro subject came up in a large group. I'm quite sure the Romans said it about the Christians, and "superior" people have been saying it about "inferiors" since man first started doing business on this planet.

"Well, do you want your daughter marryin' a Christian?"

"Go home, Junior. You're making me look silly."

Along with everybody else who gets himself mixed up in the pros and cons of racial issues in America, I have had some fun doing stuff on the Ku Klux Klan. This draws an inevitable trickle of mail, some of which expresses admiration for the "courage it takes to do such work." I drew most of these pictures in New York, where it is about as dangerous to attack the Klan as it is to come out against the man-eating shark. Of course, there

185

are Klan chapters in New Jersey, and not long ago a Pennsylvania newspaper actually printed a piece of advertising for the Klan. There are even some flapping sheets in New York State, I understand. But they are not widespread in these parts, and I don't exactly anticipate any late callers with sizzling crosses and knotted ropes. Us Nawthern upstarts can little afford to go around pinning medals on ourselves.

"Mighty nice of Brother Jenkins to lend us his store."

"Bloodstains again! And linens impossible
to find!"

The people I admire tremendously are the Southern newspapermen who have reformed in their hearts, but who approach the problem patiently, with honesty and intelligence, and are the real hope for a happy ending to the most disgraceful chapter of American history. They have guts, they are not hysterical, and they have the utmost contempt for professional agitators who are riding the Negro situation as a handy horse. Considering the way the Communist party has worked the racket for all it's worth, I think it is a great tribute to the Negro population of this country that it hasn't risen en masse to the bait. Although communism promises them little enough, our brand of Americanism has so far promised and given them even less. They are patient, and if they are cheated in the end, the rest of us deserve whatever the consequences may be.

When I first started doing a lot of cartoons about Negroes and bigotry, I was warned by the syndicate that I would probably lose most of my Southern circulation. I think it is funny as hell that while I have lost some Southern papers, the biggest number of angry and vicious letters I received, and the most cancellations I got, were from places far north of the Mason-Dixon line.

The Chinese, who once made a real science of torture, learned early that mental agony is far more excruciating than physical pain. The body provides anesthetics for racked spines and torn fingernails and burning bamboo splinters—it just makes the victim faint when the hurt becomes too great. But the brain can be tortured on and on. One of the great works of art the Chinese developed was the business of filling a bowl with water, punching a tiny hole in the bottom of the bowl, and suspending it over the bound victim's head so that drops of water fell on him every few minutes with exact regularity. Pretty soon he became a raving maniac, just waiting for the next drop to fall.

I don't think there is any better image to describe the great and liberal North's torture of minority groups, and that's why I have often wondered if it is any more humane than an old-fashioned lynching bee. In most states it is against the law to advertise resort hotels and restaurants as restricted, as people used to do. But the fact that the victims are never allowed to forget that the

188

restricted sign is there in spirit if not in print, makes you wonder if laws aren't pretty useless compared to education.

"Clannish, aren't they?"

CHAPTER X

It is a great disappointment to us bubbling young sprouts who grew up in the Franklin D. Roosevelt era when we pick up a history book and find that our enthusiasm for all sorts of star-gazing and crusading is not a new thing, that we are not blazing fresh trails for mankind to follow to its glorious destiny. Like immigration. We think of the fancy inscription on the base of the Statue of Liberty:

> Give me your tired, your poor,
> Your huddled masses yearning to breathe free,
> The wretched refuse of your teeming shore,
> Send these, the homeless, tempest-tossed, to me:
> I lift my lamp beside the golden door.

Fired by these words, we turn shudderingly to our newspapers and read about the death rattle of the Stratton Bill, which would have let 400,000 huddled characters into the country. The bubbling young sprouts feel an urge to punch congressmen in the nose, and this particular sprout draws all kinds of pictures designed to arouse

190

*George Marshall recommends legislation for entry into U. S.
of displaced persons.* News Item

the hospitable instincts of his fellow citizens. In fact,
I feel so strongly about it that once I forgot to uphold
my reputation for hating army officers; I brought my
secret admiration for George C. Marshall into the open
by doing a picture of him lighting Liberty's dead torch,

when one of his first acts as Secretary of State was to recommend the entry of DP's into America.

But us champeens of the teeming shores aren't doing a new thing. The immigration battle has been going on in this country ever since the flag had thirteen stars. Every generation for 170 years has produced two schools of thought about immigration: One has been convinced that the country has reached its saturation point, that more material for the human melting pot that produces Americans will result only in lowering the standard of living, reducing wages, and producing a crop of "furrin ideas." The other group believes—rightly, I think—that when a country reaches the stage where it can't expand its population, add new blood, and realize fresh potentialities, it might as well fold its flag because it has reached the summit and can only go downhill until it expires.

The people who belong to the current anti-immigration faction love to refer sardonically to the opposition as bleeding hearts and do-gooders and pipe-dreamers, and on most of us I guess they can make the rap stick. But they can't hang it on George C. Marshall or any of the other gents of his caliber who have certainly proved themselves immune to charges of not looking out for their country's best interests. History pretty well bears out the fact that the anti-immigration people have been the pipe-dreamers, and the other side has produced the realists.

I feel strongly enough about this to do what I cuss others for doing in different parts of this book—propagandize. Since I happen to be a citizen of this country, I would like to think of it as a living and growing thing, not as a satisfied hog interested only in wallowing in its accumulated slop and waiting for old age or the butcher's knife. I feel like doing all the propaganda I can on subjects pertaining to progressives versus moss-backs in America because picture-drawing is a reason-

"Musta been purty awful, havin' to mix with them there iggerant, uneddicated furriners."

ably lucrative trade when you're lucky enough to be syndicated, and I can already feel signs of becoming contented with my lot. I may be voting straight conservative in a few years.

I want to get all this idealistic stuff down on paper now, because after I build a house and raise a family I will be too busy supporting it and voting to protect it to be realistic about my politics. I will probably oppose immigration because a lot of excellent cartoonists live in Europe, and if one of them should sneak through Ellis Island he would not only produce work that would

OLD AMERICAN CUSTOMS: *"Here come more danged immigrants. This country is gittin' to be a dumpin' ground fer Europe's trash."*

"Careful, Pete—Pegler might hear about this."

make me and a lot of others look sick, but also he would sell it for reasonable sums and we would have to hump it twice as hard as we do to buy a new Buick every year. I might even act like that plump slob Westbrook Pegler writes admiringly about and calls "George Spelvin, American"—that typical upper-middle-class Republican, utterly contemptuous of all cultures but that of the highball and the country club, who is slowly rotting in a morass of ignorance, smugness, and sanctimony, and will find somebody else to blame when the whole blinking business comes crashing around his ears. But Pegler and his hero aren't really important. If you fear the Spelvins you can read American history and relax; if you love them you should read history and become educated. There is always a new crop of crackpots, determined to lead the country into chaos and ruin its economy, who somehow manage to save everything, including Spelvin.

When the battle between the British and the people of Palestine started hitting the front pages regularly in 1946, another war started on the inside pages of the same newspapers. A number of different Jewish factions and organizations naturally took an intense interest in the Palestine fight. Each of them had a different idea about what was right and what was wrong in Palestine, and each spent a great deal of money buying full-page newspaper ads to support its special views. The Battle of the Ads started out in a gentlemanly way, but in no time at all it had developed into a fracas fully as explosive in words, if not in deeds, as the argument between the Irgun and the British Army.

So many vituperative attacks were made upon "opposition" Jewish leaders and Jewish organizations that unless you remembered, while reading the ads, that they were written and paid for by other Jewish factions, you would have sworn you were looking at a page from the anti-Semitic publications of the late Julius Streicher.

Jews were calling other Jews warmongers, dirty liars, and bums in general. I couldn't blame any Jewish organization for feeling strongly and bitterly about some phase of the Palestine problem, nor for disagreeing with other members of his faith on the subject, but in view of the widespread anti-Semitism that already exists in America, I thought they could have done better than to wash their linen in public where their enemies could snicker at them.

Because I like to read a lot of papers, I haven't had much trouble spotting several around the East Coast that never lose a chance to display a subtle but persistent

"My, Gerald! Did you ever hear such shocking language?"

anti-Jewish bias. Every one of these papers carried its share of the ads, and it seemed terribly ironic to me that their editors, who had always feared the public indignation and shock that would result from carrying on frank and open warfare against the Jewish faith, suddenly had the opportunity to print insults to Jews right in their papers, and to make Jewish money out of the job at that.

I did a cartoon on the subject because I had learned a lesson that most people learn sooner or later if they dabble around in the field of bigotry with the idea of trying to correct some of it: Victims of bigotry can sometimes display a wide streak of it themselves, toward their own comrades, and toward other victims of persecution.

I didn't exactly expect the cartoon to make anybody think twice; the factions that were so angry they were cutting their own collective throats in paid advertisements could hardly be influenced by a piddling two-column cartoon, even if many of them saw it. But I hoped my picture would make one or two of the ad-writers wince as they were making me wince for them.

The lesson I learned about prejudice among victims of prejudice was thoroughly pounded into me by the Catholic Church shortly after I did the picture about the Zionist scrap. A rather substantial portion of the Church fell on my bean with a resounding smack after I drew some pictures about Generalissimo Francisco Franco, the boss-man of Spain. Try as I will, I somehow can't see rhyme or reason in his system—which is gaining in popularity around the world—of imprisoning, deluding, and horsewhipping citizens to protect them from communism. It smacks somewhat of paternalism, and very rugged paternalism at that. The kind that tells a man what he shall read, whom he shall talk to, and

"I wonder how long Franco is going to keep us protected from the reds!"

what he shall hear, allows him no say-so in his own affairs, takes away most of his money to pay an army to push him around, and kicks his teeth in if he talks back. Communism may be a pretty awful thing, but it would have to work hard to be any worse than the systems set up to fight it.

It has sickened me somewhat to hear Franco's setup called the last stronghold between Western Christianity and the Great Red Menace. Although I don't work hard at it, I belong to the Christian faith, and I feel insulted at the idea of being defended by a bloody-handed punk who used to lick the boots of Adolf Hitler. If Christianity ever has to depend upon Franco and his friends for protection then it will be a good time for the Church to wonder how it has failed its people so badly that there aren't enough decent ones around to support it. Christianity can't be defended by force and brutality any more than communism can be defeated by it. A lot of us kidded ourselves that fascism could be whipped that way, but all we succeeded in doing was knocking off a lot of soldiers who were on the pay rolls of the governments that espoused fascism. Sure we weakened it, but it is far from dead.

With all these notions running around in my head and all this high dudgeon in my innards, I did some pictures about Franco—one about the two old guys in jail, and one about the firing squad with Franco's propaganda poster in the background. I didn't realize how strongly certain segments of the Catholic Church felt on the subject, but I found out very quickly. I received a pile of letters that smoked with anger. When I came across

CHRISTIANITY: *The precepts and doctrines taught by Christ.* Webster's

one that called me nothing worse than a red son of a bitch, I felt positively happy, because the one preceding it was unprintable.

Then I did a drawing that really upset some folks, and the irony is that nothing was further from my mind than religious issues when I drew the thing. A number of ladies and gentlemen, who had become communists when it was more or less safe and fashionable, had recently pulled out of the party and written fascinating exposés of it. One man, who had grown up in Russia and joined the party early in that country, started the stampede by running off while working for the Soviet Purchasing Commission in Washington, and a book published under his name became a best seller. He was pretty well sponsored by Willie Hearst, who bought a lot of his stuff and who collects reformed communists by the dozen for his stable. In no time at all the magazines were full of True Confessions by ex-comrades. It became not only fashionable, but also a doggone profitable business to pull out of the dank rooms full of thick spectacles and eczema, and pop out into the bright, clean air of Free Enterprise, Unlimited.

In the caption of the cartoon, which is herewith reproduced, I used the unfortunate word "convert." Now, Webster's Unabridged has a lot of definitions for the word "convert," and its religious connotation does not appear until after a number of other meanings. You can convert your politics, or convert from coal to oil, or own a convertible car, or do lots of other kinds of converting without necessarily joining the Church. I hope the above doesn't sound flippant, but I wish to make it quite clear that I meant something besides religion when I drew a picture of two communists discussing the merits of converting.

My misfortune in the choice of words was made doubly sad by the fact that, although the cartoon had been drawn weeks before, it appeared simultaneously with the first of a series of magazine articles by Clare Boothe Luce, explaining her reasons for joining the Catholic Church. Obviously, Mrs. Luce had not been a Commie. But a fancy sum was paid for the articles (it was later announced that Mrs. Luce gave the money to a charity project), they were in a national magazine, and they were about converting (religious connotation). Also, the

"*Two magazines are competing for exclusive serial rights if we convert.*"

former managing editor of the communist *Daily Worker* had just converted (religious connotation again) with a loud bang, and was writing a series of exposés for publication. I was already suspect, I guess, because I had questioned Franco's value to the cause of Christianity in a couple of cartoons. So a lot of people put their own meaning into this one.

Several Catholic dignitaries made angry mutters about the picture, and the Brooklyn *Tablet,* which has stanchly supported Father Coughlin's Christian Front, and which suspects everybody but the toughest conservative of being a communist, ran a front-page editorial about the cartoon, with a headline stating that the New York *Herald Tribune* (a steady Republican paper) was going pink because it had printed the drawing. Several organs of the Knights of Columbus reprinted the *Tablet* editorial, and added a few choice words of their own.

It's the first time in my life I have been so roundly cussed in print, and I reacted as do most people who make a career of poking at other people and who suddenly find that they have to put up with a little of what they dish out; I didn't take it so well. I was so hopping mad that I thought of suing some of the more violently insulting sheets. I was talked out of this notion by several people who, I now suspect, were grinning up their sleeves, and I recovered after sulking behind my drawing board for a few days.

The thing that made me wild-eyed was the fact that several of the Church dignitaries and publications that called me an anti-Catholic bigot had made most unholy reputations for themselves by dealing in such truck as anti-Semitism and general venom directed against every-

204

thing left of Generalissimo Franco. It didn't matter that I had done dozens of cartoons about the Ku Klux Klan, which bitterly fights Catholicism, or that I had plumped for the entry into America of more than a million displaced persons, 65 per cent of whom were Catholic. I had criticized Franco, and I had done a drawing that appeared to make fun of some of the Church's recent and prized converts. I was a blankety-blank bigot and that was that.

After running afoul of the hard-boiled section of the Church, I figured that for a while it would be wise to give Saint Patrick's Cathedral a wide berth when my travels took me to the vicinity of Fifth Avenue and Fiftieth Street in New York City. I decided to stay clear of my Catholic stepmother and my Catholic friends for fear they would be contaminated and automatically excommunicated by my presence. My eyes nearly dropped out shortly afterward when I received a copy of a Catholic Youth publication. It ran a long story about the cartoons I was doing and said some flattering things about me. I had been under the impression that when the Church is down on you it means business, and as far as the faithful are concerned you are a pariah.

Now I pass Saint Pat's with my coat lapel turned down and my head held high, and I am at peace with the world of religion. Even if a few old mossbacks in there don't like me, I can get along with the kids.

I've been chided occasionally through the mails for doing cartoons about the Daughters of the American Revolution. The idea behind most of the complaints seems to be that a gentleman shouldn't make fun of ladies, especially distinguished and elderly ladies who

205

are proud of their ancestry and never do any harm. A couple of my relatives who belong to the organization have registered some slight disapproval, but they think I'm a nice boy and I like them, so there has never been any serious trouble over it.

My drawings about the D. A. R. started when the organization took a noisy stand against the idea of allowing 400,000 displaced persons to enter this country from Europe and fill the quota of immigrants who would normally have come into America during the four war years when the immigration service didn't do much business. Ordinarily it would just be plain funny for anybody except an American Indian to pretend to such a title as pure-blooded American, and to speak of keeping out foreign scum; but when such an attitude can mean life or death to almost half a million people, it is not so funny. Of course the D.A.R. alone couldn't make or break any big-scale immigration plans, but the dear ladies do have influence that is fairly noticeable. Most of the opposition to the legislation that would have admitted the immigrants can be written off as having been inspired by prejudice or ignorance or pure selfishness — but I can't help feeling downright mean when this ersatz aristocracy, which itself springs from foreigners and displaced persons and the "scum of Europe," gets on its high horse and tilts its nose at its own distant cousins, simply because they are separated by a few generations and a few thousand miles.

It is interesting to conjecture sometimes on what these ladies would think if their ancestors should return in all their glory and attend a D.A.R. meeting. Tattered clothing, shoeless and ragged feet, a few insects crawling in their equipment—because soldiers in the Revolution had little time to shave or attend to personal hygiene— and a shockingly radical way of talking. Imagine a troop of these weary and haggard revolutionaries standing around while the ladies recoiled in horror, then think of a Tory—a plump, rosy-cheeked Tory with his powdered wig and perfumed ruffles and lace—walking in with his sane, cultured, quiet, superior, and very, very safe and

*The battle-scarred ghost of Ezra Mulligan (Thompson's
Pennsylvania Rifle Battalion) pays a visit to his great-
great-great-great-granddaughter's D. A. R. meeting.*

conservative way of talking. Try to guess who would be
invited to stay and have tea with the Daughters of the
American Revolution—the Tory or the ancestors.

CHAPTER XI

I REMEMBER HOW GUYS IN THE ARMY USED to get angry at people back home who seemed to act very oblivious of the war sometimes. They would say they wished to hell just a few bombs could be dropped on America to give people a taste of what was going on in the rest of the world. Once in a while you would also hear a soldier remark that even people in bread lines in America had a soft time compared to the slack-bellied natives of other lands, and how fine it would be if for just one week a real famine would hit the United States, because no matter how hard you try you can't imagine starvation if you haven't lived with it.

That's all a lot of hogwash, and very few guys were serious about it. If a European or a Chinese ever learned anything from starving to death, or gained great wisdom from having his house collapse under an air raid, we have yet to hear from him. Instead of curing old hatreds, the air raids and the destruction of the last war simply piled up new scores to be settled, and all starvation has ever done is to make normally intelligent people embrace

"Nonsense, mon ami! I've been drinking on an empty stomach for seven years."

the most outlandish politics, which promise nothing but a full belly and seldom deliver even that.

But it's true that America's insulation from the cold, hard facts of life sometimes makes it incredibly blind. It's pretty trite to say that today we're an island of plenty in a sea of want, but it's true. I've done a lot of pictures about it since I've been home, not particularly because I wanted to arouse anybody's sympathies (we have sent a lot of food to Europe and this country had

"It's something silly about the last days of the Roman Empire."

a reputation for generosity long before I came on the scene with my bottle of weak ink), but because I remember the hunger I saw overseas very vividly and I am impressed by it and a little scared of it.

The fact that we have spent millions of dollars on relief for war-stricken nations isn't going to fill with

gratitude the parents whose baby is dying because
the millions didn't stretch quite far enough to include
them. They are going to hate us — not because it
was our responsibility to feed their child in the first
place, but because people in that fix can't be expected
to be rational, and any parent with a starving child is

"Allez! I'm *working this side of the street."*

"Here comes another statistic."

going to hate a man with plenty of food for purely animal reasons. To satisfy a strong hunger people will **do** anything, including murder.

I'm not really in a position to expound heavily **on** our nation's economy, or to argue many pros or cons on whether we should, for practical reasons, under-

take to feed all the rest of the world, or to let it come
to our shores. I do a lot of talking and drawing about
all these things in this book, but anybody can make a
monkey of me in an argument about them. I move along
largely by instinct on some of these matters, and right
now my instinct about the rest of the world is that even
if it means we go back to food rationing, it behooves us
to send everything edible we produce, outside of our
minimum requirements, to the starving people of the
world, whether they be communist, socialist, jingoist,
or even fascist. We should do it for our own protection,
if for no other reason.

*"It's wonderful to be liberated. Now we're
allowed to complain when we're hungry."*

It's funny that we have done nothing to any of these hundreds of millions of people who are beginning to hate us. We haven't harmed them, and in some cases we have even helped them to the extent of fighting

"In times like zis a pessimist cuts off ze slack end of his belt, while an optimist just punches anozzer hole."

their wars for them and liberating them from their oppressors. They should, under normal circumstances, admire us and love us for it. But these aren't normal circumstances. They hate us for the cave-man reason that we have plenty to eat and they don't, which is why they feel like cave men.

215

My instinct tells me that if we don't take drastic steps to fill those bellies enough so that people can think straight again, and maybe vote the kind of politics that will be best for them and for us, then we are due for something far worse than the reduction in our standard of living that such an action would cost. Our little island is going to be ringed by great multitudes of people who became terribly bitter while we haggled over the forty-hour week and the cost of Scotch whisky, and they are going to take it all away from us, and get very sick at their stomachs from cramming. I'm damned scared.

"Goody! Nylons today."

Although my general tendency toward the left in political matters sort of automatically places me on the pro-union side of the labor question, I have failed to work up a lot of steam on the subject, and have done few cartoons about it.

Even though I got as sore as anybody else overseas when reading about some wildcat strike in a war industry, I think most of us realized not only that we were getting a one-sided story, but also that for every wildcat union there was an employer somewhere who was making a good thing out of the war. Most of the boys who came home spitting fire and threatening to clonk the first union man they saw were inclined that way before the war.

I will admit that my rather passive attitude toward the big labor-union argument in America is largely due to the fact that my postwar life has enabled me to afford the luxury of being abstract about it. My daily bread has been assured, unions or no unions. In this remote frame of mind, I feel very strongly against punitive measures such as the Taft-Hartley bill, which make all labor unions pay a stiff penalty for the excesses of some bad unions—but I don't find it hard to see why the bill didn't arouse the ire of the nation as a whole, and why Taft's popularity and unpopularity hasn't changed a great deal because he was one of the bill's authors. Among many honest craftsmen in skilled trades there is resentment against unions because when some workers are overprotected they become sloppy and careless. Among civil service people and others whose incomes are fixed at an adequate level in normal times, but who suffer immensely when prices go up, there is a

217

"Why didn't somebody tell me we're gonna strike? I been buyin' stock in the doggone company."

great deal of anger at the fact that an unskilled laborer makes twice as much money as a man who holds a job that took years of study, education, and heartbreaking work. To people who feel a great concern about the condition of the rest of the world and the future of our nation in it, it seems rather ridiculous that so much time and effort should be spent worrying about an extra hour's work at time and a half, and that people working at jobs essential to the rebuilding of the world should strike when their lot is far above that of even the most fortunate persons in foreign lands.

But this is a hard-boiled world, and it's pretty obvious that labor unions have become toughened and tempered by decades of dealing with various employers, many of whom are rather unscrupulous gents. If the unions were suddenly to become starry-eyed and full of emotion and

"I had to walk to work. The doggone bus drivers are on strike."

agree to work harder at longer hours until the economy of the nation and the world was straightened out, their opponents would lose no time in taking advantage of the situation. I prefer to keep out of the whole thing and

"The union was pleased with that full-page ad about Amalgamated Steel. Now Amalgamated wants us to do one about the union."

think about other matters. I am quite sure labor unions and their opponents can get along fine and do a good job of looking out for themselves without any aid from the likes of me.

While messing around in amateur politics after the war, I did a lot of cartoons about the Dies Committee in Congress. When I pinned labels on the figures in some of the cartoons, I could never be quite sure whether the outfit called itself the House Committee on Un-American Affairs, the Committee to Investigate Un-American Activities, or the House Un-American Activities Committee. It was referred to by a different title each time in the papers, and I used most of the labels at one time or another, so I'm sure I was right at least once or twice. But whether or not I put the words of the jawbreaking title in their proper order, I tried to convey the impression that I was in complete agreement with one of the few real communists the Committee has succeeded in nailing, when he said, upon being convicted of contempt of Congress for refusing to respect a subpoena by the Committee, that he most certainly was contemptuous of the Un-American Activities section of the House of Representatives. The convicted gentleman behaved in general like an ass, but his inquisitors on the Committee were such monstrously greater asses that they actually made him look like a martyr.

The Committee was started by a Texas congressman named Martin Dies, who professed a great fear of communism many years ago, and who felt that such agencies as the FBI and the city and state police weren't doing a very good job of exposing the Red Menace in America.

"Hot ziggety! A real one at last!"

They were slightly restricted by an old and wrinkled piece of paper known as the Bill of Rights, which forbids cops the privilege of pushing a man around solely because of his political beliefs. While Dies could find nothing in the stodgy old Constitution or the Bill of Rights that allowed Congress to set up its own Gestapo, he couldn't find anything that specifically forbade it either—possibly because the founders of this country didn't dream such things as the Great Red Menace were in the offing. So Congress allowed the Texan to form his committee, and the House of Representatives has steadily voted funds for its operations ever since, to the everlasting shame of everybody connected with it. One of the chairmen of the Committee who succeeded Dies was John Rankin, the Mississippian who has distinguished himself as one of the cleverest gutter-fighters

"Read 'em? I'm too busy protectin' 'em to read 'em."

who ever flapped a lip in the halls of Congress. His remarks about fellow humans, recorded in the *Congressional Record,* make the bigoted ravings of such buffoons as Senator Bilbo or Elizabeth Dilling sound like a child's rendition of the Lord's Prayer.

A friend of mine named Mike Monroney, who is a congressman from Oklahoma and whom I have liked

"I wondered where he was learning all that bad language."

and admired for several years, once took me to a party
in Washington that was attended by most of the Democrat dignitaries in Congress, and I had the opportunity
of observing the social behavior of Rankin, and the attitude his colleagues have toward him. The place was

packed with Southern Democrats, most of whom share Rankin's general views on race, religion, and politics, but many of whom feel that way simply because of upbringing and tradition and not because of venom toward humanity in general. Rankin was the loneliest man I ever saw at a party. Although several colleagues greeted him in passing, not one tarried for conversation, and the jabbering groups that formed around the cocktail and canapé tables became strangely silent when he passed them.

No doubt his ostracism by the more or less decent elements of his fellow lawmakers has intensified his bitterness toward people in general. But his associates don't laugh at him as they used to at his fellow Mississippian, Bilbo, whom they considered reasonably harmless (!) and empty-headed. Rankin is nicknamed "The Killer," because few congressmen, even experienced tongue-crackers, have been able to outargue or outlegislate him, and those who have tangled with him have generally come out losers.

He used to be quite a dashing guy, who fought hard for a lot of good causes and was considered somewhat radical, of all things — although he never qualified as a left-winger. Even recently he has shown a marked interest in assisting deserving people. Rankin is the man most responsible for the bill raising the pay of the army private from the ridiculous sum of $21 a month to $50, and on several occasions he has supported General Omar Bradley at a time when Bradley sorely needed help in his program for veterans' welfare.

But those are about the only lilies growing out of the dung pile which is John Rankin's political record in

225

recent years. During his service as chairman of the House Committee on Un-American Activities, he has used his prestige and immunity as a congressman to persecute, insult, and embarrass scores of far better citizens than himself, few of whom were communists. And he has publicly committed violations of basic human rights

"Investigate them? Heck, that's mah posse."

"Do you mean your American way or my American way, Senator?"

that would long ago have landed him in the pokey had he tried the same tricks as a private citizen. While he has behaved more like a Gestapo agent than an American toward members of any political group other than his own extreme right wing, he has never once voiced disapproval of or investigated individuals or organizations that deal professionally in religious or racial bigotry (many of them going to the extreme of spilling blood, as in the case of the Ku Klux Klan). His group, which considers itself a watchdog of Americanism, has always stuck its tongue in its cheek and ignored the antics of all lunatics who commit violence in the name of white supremacy or Christian America, and who for the most part showed a marked sympathy toward the enemy during the last war because the ideals set forth in *Mein Kampf* had a tremendous appeal for them. By all this, the Committee has plainly implied that there is only one kind of un-Americanism — that of the left wing. So long as you vote the "right" ticket you can be any kind of bastard and there is no question of your patriotism or your behavior in the eyes of the Committee members or their new chairman, a New Jersey Republican named Thomas, who replaced the Democrat Rankin in 1946.

A great number of left-wing people whom I have joined in cussing the Committee have confined their complaints to the fact that the congressional Gestapo picks on the left wing and doesn't hound the lunatic fringes of the right wing. I have pointed up the Committee's noncritical and sometimes downright sympathetic attitude toward American fascism in my drawings, but only because I think that is what makes it look most ridiculous. The attitude of some lefties seems as one-sided to me as the attitude of the congressmen they hate. I'm quite sure a lot of them would be perfectly happy to see the Committee function as it does, if only it would transfer its attentions from the left wing to the right wing. The attitude of these same lefties toward oppressive leftist governments abroad and their heated defense of the Kremlin's right to butcher political opponents bears this out.

Most of the strange political organizations with which I managed to involve myself after getting out of the army, struck me as being intolerant on the one hand while preaching equality and brotherly love on the other. One of the few exceptions has been the Civil Liberties Union (not to be confused with the extremely partisan Civil Rights Congress, which has been suspected, of devising the name to create such confusion).

Freedom's brave sentinels.

"I could do a good job on these here enemies o' democracy if I didn't hafta worry about th' dang voters!"

After pulling myself off a number of letterheads and committees, and moping around with a bellyful of the phonies whose only objection to nondemocratic procedures was when such procedures didn't suit their plans, I read an item about how the Civil Liberties Union had defended the right of the Communist party to exist on a Midwestern state ballot, and had in the same week defended the right of Gerald L. K. Smith, the bush-league Mussolini, to speak in a municipal auditorium that had been denied him by authorities in a city in another state. It was sort of like seeing a light through the fog.

This sounds pretty snippy in print, and I don't love clichés very much, but I was beginning to think that if you are going to snort around about freedom and all that stuff, it has to work both ways. While I don't feel like laughing the Gerald Smiths off as harmless demagogues, I don't see how anyone can honestly claim the right of free assembly and speech for himself while denying it to others. As long as Smith doesn't violate existing criminal laws, he can stir up his revolution just as the Commies are stirring up theirs. And the congressional Gestapo has no business fooling with him, even if it felt like it, which isn't likely. I became a paid-up member of the Civil Liberties Union, which puts out leaflets expressing the above sentiments a hell of a lot better than I have done. I have always disliked professional joiners who walk lopsided from the weight of miscellaneous membership cards in their wallets. But any outfit I can find these days that opposes peanut heads in powerful places who think the way to keep the Founding Fathers resting quietly in their graves is to liquidate political opposition, is going to get my five bucks as long as I have it to spend.

CHAPTER XII

People who, like myself, feel bitterly toward American citizens who subscribed to Hitler's ideologies at home while the army was abroad fighting Hitler's soldiers are often inclined to forget themselves and advocate the suppression of the offenders. I can't recall how many times I have been approached by people who wanted me to sign my name to statements calling for the prosecution of such people as Gerald Smith. One group actually wanted to petition the government to suppress William Randolph Hearst's papers and the McCormick-Patterson publications. Not all the groups organized for such purposes were politically left of center, no matter how much the objects of their hatred would like to think of them as a pack of mangy communists. Many were just private citizens and veterans outraged by the fact that some newspapers during the war were far more sympathetic toward the German cause than our own, and yet had the unmitigated gall to profess intense patriotism and 100 per cent Americanism.

I have never lost an opportunity to take cracks at the

"Must be election time. Ze government ees building ze opposition party's platform."

above-named newspapers, and once chortled with glee when Gerald Smith was tossed into the klink by a Chicago judge on a legitimate charge of misbehavior. But in view of the drawings I have done in defense of the Communist party's right to exist, I would be guilty of hypocrisy if I put my name on a piece of paper advocating anybody's suppression for his political activities so long as he stayed within the framework of the laws against sedition.

It has been argued that Hearst, McCormick, Patterson, and some of the lesser lights in the same camp were all guilty of giving aid and comfort to the enemy in wartime. I remember seeing several German propaganda leaflets, shot over our lines in Europe, that quoted and gave credit to the New York *Daily News,* the Chicago *Tribune,* and various Hearst writers. But if a jury were summoned to decide whether the publishers were guilty, I would be disqualified to sit on it because my views are prejudiced in favor of the other side of the political fence from theirs. I would be all too inclined to decide the verdict long before the lawyers finished talking. Besides, such a jury has not been called and probably never will be. Nobody has the right to ask for the suppression of such people, but I certainly intend to make the most of my right to call them every name under the sun. If they are eventually put out of business by the people who can really do it — their readers and advertisers — I will be only too happy to watch it happen.

By the same token, I have no sympathy for any communist who is found guilty of breaking an existing law against sedition or any other criminal activity. But my strong objection to such organizations as the House Committee on Un-American Activities is based on the fact that few of its victims are accused of any legal offense, and therefore have no opportunity to defend themselves as in a court of law (you can't talk back to

Congress). They emerge from their investigations with their reputations as besmirched as if they had been convicted of criminal acts. For example, they are charged with owing their primary loyalty to an outside power.

The sportsman.

It can hardly be denied that a real Commie's first loyalty belongs to the party, which has its roots in Russia. Yet nearly all Americans are guilty, if such a thing is a crime. Everybody who worships God is putting an outside power above his country, and certainly every devout Catholic owes obedience to the Pope, who is the recognized chief of a foreign state and who even has an army of his own.

Communism is a religion, and a fanatic one, to its adherents, and our Intelligence and Security people would be delinquent if they failed to keep a sharp eye on the Communist party should such a thing as a war with Russia come about, just as they watched the German-American

"Yer a menace to the people. It's me duty to sink your end of the boat."

Bund during the last war. But so long as there is no war, no agency or committee should be allowed to violate the constitutional rights of any group of Americans, regardless of their political or religious affiliations. At least not in the name of Americanism.

Thomas Jefferson, who is generally regarded by historians as a fairly important early American with unquestionable loyalty to his nation, is the author of this remark: "If there be any among us who wish to dissolve this Union or to change its republican form, let them stand undisturbed, as monuments of the safety with which error of opinion may be tolerated where reason is

"Careful, Grandma — that's the first step toward fascism."

left free to combat it." There could be no better reason for dissolving the House Committee on Un-American Activities, or for Americans in general to cease and desist from the monstrous witch hunt that has developed since the end of the war.

No American, whether he be a newspaper publisher, a politician, a businessman, or whatever, can morally defend his own freedom of opinion once he has advocated the loss of another man's. No leftie who has picketed and rioted at neo-fascist gatherings has the right to complain when the same thing happens to him. And certainly Bertie McCormick, who has probably done more than any other American to demand suppression of political opposition, has no right to trumpet about freedom of the press as he does every hour on the hour.

I wish I were capable of writing brilliant and witty things about suppression. It has been one of my favorite cartoon subjects, and I have covered everything from the Dies Committee to the Boston book-banning people, whom I once portrayed clustered around a risqué volume with their eyes popping out, obviously intending to read every single page of the evil thing before declaring it unfit for public consumption.

And I took a great deal of pleasure in doing a picture about one of the greatest ironies of our conquest over Germany — the fact that several enthusiastic American and British army officers took it upon themselves to tell some Germans what books they could and could not own. Since the former government had already cleaned out all but the most pro-Nazi literature, this new measure pretty well wiped out their libraries. The Germans, who have always been very morbid about their humor, must

"Nothing left but nursery rhymes, Herr Schlinker. My library has been purified by Hitler and decontaminated by the Allies."

have considered the whole thing a classic joke.

I think my drawings about the great postwar sport of red-baiting got me into more trouble with the papers who bought my stuff, and the people who read it, than did anything else. I remember seeing one of those Washington newsletters list me along with several other people as a fellow traveler. Of course, I did knock out a few pictures that weren't exactly flattering to the extreme left wing; although I felt much more in sympathy with the left than with the right, I couldn't resist the wonderful

Fellow travelers.

Portrait of some prewar isolationists...now.

cartoon material offered from time to time by the flexible
American Communist party, which was rapidly returning
to its prewar isolationist stand now that our intervention
in foreign affairs conflicted with the policies of Russia.

It has been very funny, even to nonexpert political
observers like myself, to watch the extreme right and
the extreme left turn their isolationism on and off like a
water tap. Many America Firsters, who, when Germany
was riding high, declared that we should attend strictly
to our own business because Hitler's conquests did not
endanger us, now became terribly concerned about
Russia's expansion and advocated all sorts of drastic

"Darling! Then you didn't mean it when you left me in 1940!"

steps, including war, to stop her. But the Commies take all prizes for speed in policy-changing. Russia feared Hitler at first, and the party in America was ready to fight at the drop of a hat. Then Germany and Russia signed their big-brother pact early in the war, and the *Daily Worker's* subscribers were informed that the Nazis really meant well at heart, and anybody who questioned their motives should be shot as a war-mongering skunk. When Hitler attacked Russia, the comrades who had picketed our war-mongering factories dropped their sandwich boards and asked for work to help in the great

242

war for humanity. And now they are picketing again.

Although the comrades say that any criticism of them is red-baiting, just as the fanatics on the other side call all dissenters communist-inspired, there is a great difference between red-baiting and sincere criticism. Once I had a fine long talk with a friend who is not a party member but who might as well be one, since he unswervingly follows the official line of the party. During the talk he assured me that true communists have a delightful sense of humor, and are most responsive to constructive criticism about their activities. I asked him what he considered constructive criticism. He wrinkled his brow, then replied with a burst of words which, when filtered through my gray matter, defined constructive criticism as nondestructive criticism. He offered no examples. I gave him a whole list of criticisms that have been made of the Soviet Union, and he knocked each aside as destructive red-baiting.

People who are well indoctrinated in communist methods of discussion have a wonderful system for putting their opponents on the defensive, and the few times I have undertaken to argue with one of them I have been soundly beaten down. Instead of answering questions, they counter with other questions. Instead of defending themselves against accusations, they make counteraccusations. The most popular defense against remarks about Soviet detention camps for political opponents is to remind the critic of the lynchings in our own South. The answer to the charge of Soviet imperialism is that we took our own country away from the Indians. When even minor party members and sympathizers can parry, feint, and bull their way out of tight corners in argu-

243

ments without ever giving a satisfactory reply to any statement, then surely nobody can blame any diplomat who is soundly defeated and deflated by such a high-ranking party man as Andrei Gromyko.

If you have the opportunity to be around many people of strong and varying political opinions, once in a while you are treated to a wonderful spectacle—an argument between a veteran pro-Russian and a veteran red-baiter of the old school. The scene never lasts long, because there are always goody-goodies who pull them apart, but it is elegant while it is going on. Both are extremely pig-

"... *where ignorance is bliss, 'tis folly to be wise.*"

headed, and both spout worn clichés with a color and a vehemence that almost make them sound brand new. And both are very much alike in that each has developed a skull six inches thick to prevent any new ideas from entering.

If the power of suppression were not available to professional red-baiters, and they would confine their activities to throwing verbal brickbats at bona fide communists, I don't think any harm would be done by it. And it would be doggone entertaining, because a head-butting contest between two billy goats is amusing to spectators and harmless to the belligerents. But the baiters are having things pretty much their own way these days, after a long period of frustration, and they are striking wildly in all directions and are liable to do heavy damage to a lot of people, including themselves. These days, anybody who voted for and believed in Roosevelt; any history teacher who tries to be objective about events of the past and to include a little deserved criticism of our own behavior and a little honest praise for some of the constructive things about socialism; or any newspaper or radio commentator who questions the current American foreign policy, is suspected and accused of pro-Soviet inclinations, and stands a damn good chance of being investigated, insulted, and fired. People with new ideas, or those who step out of the popular line of thought, have always been lambasted as crackpots and radicals. Sometimes they have been exactly that, but quite often they have accomplished great things, and certainly none of the advances made in civilization has been due to counterrevolutionaries and advocates of the status quo.

"Danged crackpot radical!"

It is going to be an awful thing if the stanch conservatives in America succeed in labeling and banishing everything left of center, because their joy will be very short-lived, and everybody will suffer for it. Not only will a lot of undeserving characters be decorated with the glamorous halos of martyrs, but the country will stagnate for want of new ideas, because few progressives can be found in the ranks of the hidebound and fearful.

When the Soviet government recently completed one of its many purges in occupied countries of alleged conspirators against the people, and at the same time announced that henceforth it was largely going to do away with capital punishment for state offenses, I did a drawing showing two Russian jailers about to help their prisoner

"There's nothing to it, Excellency. Comrade Popoff and I have committed hundreds of successful suicides."

hang himself and so officially commit suicide. Not having been an eyewitness to such a procedure, I couldn't do the drawing from experience, but only on conjecture. I based it on reports from many sources, but because it wasn't anything I'd seen, I won't try to defend myself if anybody accuses me of doing a little red-baiting. I think I know why local communists can truly call almost any criticism of Russian behavior red-baiting.

Observers and newspapermen are pretty well restricted in Russia. Some of them have traveled rather widely in the Soviet Union, but thus far few have gone home with a firsthand report of the workings of the Soviet penal system. They don't know much about it unless they have run afoul of it and been in the can themselves, in which case they seldom go home at all. Of course, there are a few ex-Soviets kicking around in America and elsewhere who have been through the mill, but so many of them have discovered the commercial advantages of telling almost any kind of story and having it believed that it is hard to know which ones to trust. I think it is safer to assume that, since Russia is a one-party state which tolerates no political opposition, it treats its political prisoners exactly as has every totalitarian state in history, and we certainly have abundant evidence of what the others have done. Until a man turns up with proof that he openly opposed the government in Russia and escaped with nothing more than a rap on the wrist and a gentle admonition, I think such an attitude is reasonably fair. The Russian government itself has occasionally admitted scragging a few opposition leaders, and has never denied that it is willing to toss a man in the klink for talking out of the wrong side of his mouth.

"It's a new system. We give each rebel a confession and one of those new Yankee fountain pens, then we hold him under until he signs."

Every once in a while I receive a letter from a gent who favors everything the Soviet does, and he tells me what an idealistic young man I am to oppose suppression of the Communist party. Then occasionally I get letters from the same gent telling me what a cynic I am for drawing the conclusion that Russia knocks its political prisoners around. Actually, I have just tried to be consistent. Some people think on very elevated planes and in complicated ways, and can see nothing illogical about praising free political activity and justifying totalitarianism in Russia. We have these complicated thinkers on the right as well as on the left. Many people see nothing wrong with yipping about a free press in America and defending Franco or Perón, who have quaint, if unoriginal, ways of dealing with opposition newspapers and politicians.

The excuse generally given for that kind of logic is this: The lefties say the Russian people aren't yet ready to think for themselves and must be led by the hand for a while. The rightists say Franco and Perón are faced with the Red Menace which is out to destroy their fine institutions and their churches, and they must keep an iron control over politics or they will be ruined. Few of these apologists, right or left, stop to think that they are admitting the tremendous appeal the opposition must have for the people in those countries; otherwise there would be no reason to control everybody so rigidly.

The people who so justify Russia's system are certainly most flattering to Americans when they call them almost the only people on earth capable of governing themselves. I've seen a lot of this country, North, South, and middlewise, in my youthful travels, and somehow I'm struck with the impression that there are an awful lot of dummies exercising the privilege of dropping a ballot in a box, but a lot more people who have a pretty good idea of what they are about. A great part of the world's population would learn very quickly how to govern **if** given the chance. But I don't have a missionary complex about it, and I don't think our magnificent nation has the right to try to make over the world in its own

"I'm sorry, comrade. I didn't know we'd stopped hating Argentina."

image; lots of nations are rather critical of our system and prefer their own ways of doing things.

I don't draw my little red-baiting pictures about the insides of Russian jails to help bring about any counter-revolutions in that country, but just because the possible naïveté that causes me to make pictures about the rights of the Communist party in the United States also causes me to make the jail pictures. I like free living, and I don't think there is a Messiah, a Leader, or a Planner alive whose system or regime gives results worth the loss of personal freedom.

When I was looking over the pile of cartoons that went into this book, and selecting those about Russia for this section, I was struck by the fact that I have done far fewer anti-Russian drawings than anti-anti-Russian ones. Every time I start work on a drawing about what I consider Russia's misbehavior, I shrink inwardly because I think of all the sons of bitches in this country who are doing the same thing for reasons of their own, and I often throw the drawing away. I think my definition of a real red-baiter is a man who opposed the Russian revolution from the start, who opposes the idea of every revolution that ever occurred, who would have opposed our own revolution had it happened in his time, and is strictly in favor of the lousy masses staying in their muddy places where they belong instead of running around taking pot shots at refined aristocrats who were born to rule, even if they were born slightly syphilitic and sadistic. Such a man is responsible for bringing about the revolutions he abhors because he clings so tightly to the status quo and opposes so bitterly even the mildest social advances that eventually the people

Ex-dogface who owns Russian battle decoration.

who would have been happy with gradual improvement in their lot come running over his lawn, shoot up his family, and break into his wine cellar to get stinking drunk and proclaim themselves masters of themselves. I'm not wild about revolutions either. I have met a few revolutionaries and think they are awful punks who found it so hard to get along with the rest of society that they want to run it themselves. On the other hand, I don't mean to be so reactionary I help to bring revolutions about. I don't like the thought of little kids and old ladies swimming around in their own blood just because they are a rich man's relatives.

It has been pointed out that the only thing the planners of the Russian revolution forgot, while arranging the best way for people to get along, was human nature. I think a single example of what has occurred with the original planners hardly cold in their graves, suffices to prove that point: The Soviet laws have been revised so that it is now possible to inherit money in Russia. The gents who yelled that one of the worst aspects of capitalism was the dynasties formed by families who passed booty along from lazy generation to lazier generation, would yell even louder if they were alive to see this happen. So now the representatives of the proletariat are going to pass their titles and their fortunes right down the line, and we know who will be the future leaders of the proletariat—even if they too are born syphilitic, sadistic, and filthy rich.

I remember that my pride in my own army—I did have a little—was slightly offended when I saw some postwar Russian textbooks that taught Soviet school kids the Russian Army won the war with only a little token support from the rest of the Allies. I know they suffered millions more casualties than we did and incalculably more damage than anybody else, but they would have had a hell of a time without us. Besides, we were practically committed to the war, for reasons far less immediate than anybody else's, at a time when they were

"I'll bet a million you're wrong, Comrade Kovinski—figuratively speaking, of course."

still playing footie with the Germans. I believe in giving them full credit for their accomplishments, which were many; but I lost a lot of friends by German bullets that otherwise would have been fired at Russians, and I am still living close enough to the war to resent, for purely chauvinistic reasons, any insult to my late friends.

The Russians can take cracks at my country if they

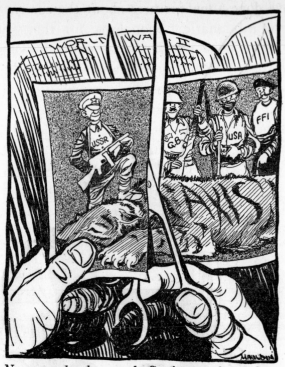

New textbooks teach Soviet students how Russian Army won with little aid from Allies.
News Item

feel like it; it deserves considerable criticism, and we have thrown more than our fair share of insults at them in the past. But I don't want them teaching their kids that my friends in graves overseas all died in automobile accidents. I have made profane sounds and come close to getting my nose bloodied several times when somebody pooh-poohed Russia's war effort and said she'd never have accomplished anything without a lot of good old free-enterprise, lend-lease equipment. I don't think you can be derisive about dead soldiers, and the Russians buried a lot.

256

I have done a few pictures about the current Russian trend toward fanatic nationalism, for that stuff leads to war. I've done ten times as many drawings about our own brand of 100 per cent American slob, because blind obedience to a state that is made into a god is the thing responsible for most of the world's past troubles. The Russians claim they are doing it because we are doing it, and vice versa, but I think there is a little more danger from Russian nationalism because they are better equipped for it. If the Kremlin says you are 100 per cent Russian you are 100 per cent Russian or you are a forgotten Russian. In America there are always a few

"This is just for expediency. You mustn't forget you're a socialist at heart."

MAULDIN

subversives who talk back. So maybe if I am going to
do pictures on the subject I should reverse the proportion and do ten about them for one about us. But then,
I live here, and it is more fun to draw the pictures about
home.

I did two cartoons about Andrei Gromyko, who lives
about fifteen blocks from me in New York on the classy
side of Park Avenue. I'll admit the drawings were a
little unfair; I did them on the standard of living that
Gromyko, the champion of the masses, is enjoying in

258

New York. After all, he is a diplomatic representative of a major nation, and as such can hardly be expected to live in squalor. I laid off him when he was living on the fabulous Mills estate on Long Island, where it costs $30,000 a year just to keep the grounds in shape. But I

"It says Comrade Gromyko's New York residence is in an overcrowded slum known as the Park Avenue district."

felt he lost his diplomatic immunity to jibes when, clad in a dress suit, he strolled into the Waldorf-Astoria one evening, right through a picket line of deserving working-men who were striking for better wages.

I did another red-baiting job when, one evening late in October, 1946, I sat curled around a venomous book by some Trotskyite or other, who was explaining in detail how the Russians, when occupying a new country, always go after the noncommunist left wing and purge it long before they start on the capitalists. He claimed that real communists fear and hate nothing more than independent labor movements, social reformers, and other lily-livered pinkos whose ambitions for a new society stop short of spilling blood. He claimed that real communists can understand and even grudgingly admire a hardheaded old reactionary because they can predict him and outmaneuver him, but that they can't abide an independent thinker who might vomit at the thought of digesting some of the official party dogma, and who might even think he has a better way of doing things than the party. The author published an alleged copy of a directive issued to Soviet commanders during the occupation of Poland, giving them a list of priorities for political purges. Right at the top of the list were all the socialist, reformist, and various intellectual groups. Then followed labor leaders. Then a few Communist party members who might be suspected of having ideas of their own. And right at the bottom were the imperialists, royalists, capitalists, and assorted oppressors of the people. I found this book a little hard to swallow and was about to dismiss it from my mind and return it to its owner when the radio announced that a Moscow broadcast had asked America, as a favor to its great friend and ally Russia, to vote for all the November candidates that were approved by the PAC.

It was a kiss of death if I ever knew one. The Russians act amazingly oblivious of the opinions of other people sometimes. But with all the important Russian newspaper-

Moscow broadcast pats PAC on back. October headline

men, observers, and politicians who were kicking around in America (as well as their sources of information among native Americans), they couldn't have failed to know that the worst possible thing Russia could do to a politician in this country would be to endorse him openly. This was like something right out of the book. I sat and thought about it for a long time before making the cartoon. Whether the book's author was right or wrong, and whether Moscow's radio did the stunt stupidly or deliberately, the cartoon was still accurate.

Chapter XIII

UNITED FEATURE SYNDICATE BECAME VERY worried about the path I seemed to be treading with all my drawings about red-baiting and race relations. The former had become a delicate subject for newsprint, and the latter has always been something smart syndicates keep away from, because there are thousands of newspapers in areas where racial prejudice is strong, and each of them is a prospective client who must not be offended. It was explained to me by the syndicate, in a tone reserved for backward children and young men with stirrings of a social conscience, that selling cartoons on a nation-wide basis was a business designed to produce a handsome and steady income for both artist and distributor, and that it was damn poor business I was doing.

The syndicate manager who took over after George Carlin's death explained carefully to me that he himself felt strongly in favor of some of the things I was doing, and he wanted me to understand that all the other syndicate people in the business office, the sales office, and elsewhere, must not be regarded as callous souls without

"Right now we're nursing him through a bad siege of social-consciousness."

a glimmering of warmth toward high ideals and social reforms. But, he said, this was a business, and businessmen can't be politicians. One of the syndicate editors was much more plain-spoken. "If you're gonna do that kind of crap," he said, "you should stop doing syndicated work and ask for a job at the *New Masses* or the *Daily Worker.*"

I was losing papers at a terrific pace. During one period my loss averaged one paper a day. The syndicate stopped trying to reason with me and started butchering the drawings as they came in. In the five years I had been in the army, working part time for the *45th Division News* for three years and full time for *Stars and Stripes* for two years, I had turned out hundreds upon hundreds of cartoons, most of which took one kind of dirty crack or another at the army and its ways. The army is by necessity a totalitarian system, which makes no pretense of allowing freedom of speech or behavior; yet in five years only three of my drawings had been stopped. Each of the three contained background sketches of equipment I had noticed in the field overseas and hadn't known was new stuff that, for security reasons, could not be described in words or pictures. I remember one of the pictures was of a new tank destroyer. In other words, my army censorship had been for stern and logical security reasons, and never once for policy. Several gents of high rank had tried to have the cartoons emasculated, but there were always other gents of equal rank who felt the stuff I was doing was justified.

In the first year after my discharge from the army and my introduction into civilian life in the land of the free and the stronghold of an independent press, I had done about two hundred drawings — only a fraction of my army production — and more than forty of the two hundred had been censored by the syndicate. One example is included near by — the one about the senator offering his home town for a UN site. This was drawn at the time when it looked as if UN was going to have to settle on a Pacific Island because nobody seemed to want to give it any space. A friend had written to me with the suggestion that I do a drawing on the irony of UN, with all its multicolored delegates, deciding to settle in a land that

"About holding United Nations conferences in your home town, Senator — you may all be 100 per cent Americans, but you see, United Nations includes other 100 per cent nationalities too."

"About your home town's offer to let United Nations hold its conferences there, Senator — don't you think the Abyssinian delegation might object to riding the back seats of the busses?"

practices Jim Crow. The original caption and the substitute written by the syndicate editor are both under the drawing.

I don't think I would have objected quite so strongly had the substitute captions made any sense, but after looking at the horrible things I decided I was not only being censored unmercifully, but was being sabotaged as well. Several other drawings scattered through this book also underwent blue-pencil operations, but they have simply been restored to their original shape without any comment.

During my censorship battles with the syndicate, they used to raise hell about my using real names in cartoons. While Senator Bilbo was a subject of wide discussion around the country, I did several pictures about him, but was never allowed to spell his name out. I was told that he might sue, in spite of the fact that during that period it was quite fashionable to bang him around in print. Even writers who had always observed the utmost caution about offending any possible customers with cracks at well-known bigots, made cracks at Bilbo and erected a halo of liberalism above their heads. The man just didn't seem to have any friends, and so it looked safe. I agreed with people who said that the Bilbos on earth thrive on any kind of publicity, good or bad, and that he shouldn't be portrayed as a holy terror, because it dignified and flattered him. But I did enjoy making fun of him, and I didn't like not being able to spell his name.

Then one day I did a drawing about Jimmy Petrillo, who had said or done something that didn't appeal to me. Just for the hell of it, I spelled the union leader's name out, and was very surprised when it got by the

*"I'll sue th' bums! They misspelled my
name!"*

syndicate's blue-pencil boys without a single alteration.
I asked them if they weren't afraid of a law suit, and
evidently they had forgotten about the Bilbo argument,
because they said, "Not a chance. Everybody hates him."
I do not mean to imply that the syndicate loved Bilbo
and tried to protect him; their censorship has never
seemed particularly biased to me. It's just that every
paper howls at Petrillo, while a few might possibly sym-
pathize secretly with Bilbo and be scared away from
buying my cartoons because I made fun of him.

The complaints from angry editors followed two general trends. The most common was, "We bought the kid's stuff for entertainment. We have our own editorial cartoonist." The other was, "We thought he was going

"Maybe if one of us went down and talked to Petrillo . . ."

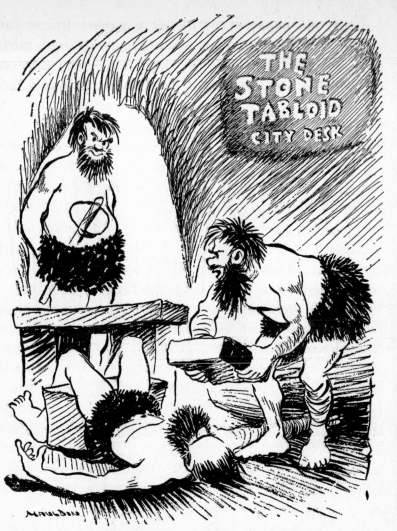

"Next time you write a letter to the editor, hand it to him."

to draw veteran pictures, not become a bumbling world reformer." There were other editors who didn't object to my politics, but who were disappointed in the quality of many of the cartoons. Every time I heard from one of these, I felt completely in agreement with him, because

I wasn't too happy about my work either. But so far as the editors who disliked my politics were concerned, I felt they should either drop the cartoons and take on something more to their liking, or else run the stuff and let me alone.

Actually, I found myself in a vicious circle. I hadn't wanted to start drawing cartoons immediately on becoming a civilian, because I knew I would be unable to turn out really good pictures. The celebrity stuff I have described had balled me up, and when you are confused you just can't do decent work. I was a rookie at being a civilian, and knew nothing of the multitude of little civilian problems that make ideal cartoon material. I couldn't qualify as a typical veteran and certainly hadn't lived the life of one, so I was unable to do clear and simple pictures about most veteran troubles and experiences. This left me with little to draw about but my feelings about postwar politics and our relations with the rest of the world, about which I felt very strongly. My qualifications to do such work are open to serious question, but my feelings were quite sincere and very intense. And after looking over the vast numbers of quacks who make a business of peddling political opinions, I felt I could hold my head above the worst of them and perhaps someday learn as much as some of the better ones.

But I didn't want to draw so blinking much political stuff, and the syndicate had forced me, by not letting me take a few months off to get my feet on the ground, into doing the very thing that was getting me into trouble and costing them profits. The more the syndicate censored me and the more the editors complained, the more defiant I got. Pretty soon I found myself doing nothing

271

but straight political drawings, and very bad ones at that, because instead of trying to be clever or subtle I said to hell with everybody, and I climbed on a soapbox and let fly with a sledge hammer, when I should have used a needle. Cartoons are no good if they are soapboxy and pontifical. They have to be thrust gently, so that the victim doesn't know he's stabbed until he has six inches of steel in his innards.

Any child learns early in life that defiance gets you no place. I had learned it, but I had to learn it all over again. I was sore at the syndicate and at the group of editors who were complaining because I was drawing pictures with a political slant instead of entertaining ones. Most of the editors had evidently never realized that my war cartoons, which they had bought during the tremendous flurry of publicity I received, were never intended to be funny, but had all been drawn with a slant. I was so sore I kept on turning out the kind of picture that cost me a whale of a lot of papers that had understood my stuff, liked it sincerely, and had been prepared to continue printing my output for a long time in the future.

I didn't realize what I was doing to myself until the St. Louis *Post-Dispatch,* which is one of the truly great papers of America and is noted for its fairness, its sincerity, and its open-mindedness, and which had been one of my very first subscribers, canceled its contract for my drawings. That stopped me dead in my tracks like nothing else could have. Until then I could sit around with my buddies and console myself with the ancient, lame excuse that my rapid downhill slide was due to the fact that there is no such thing as freedom of opinion in this land of dirty old reactionaries, that the press is a tool of the National Association of Manufacturers, and generally dream up a wonderful series of plausible reasons for not trying to improve the quality of my work.

I can't abide the self-styled martyrs of the left wing who wail about the reactionary press in America, and the difficulty of getting any nonconservative material printed outside of the few publications that are frankly leftish themselves, with leftish readership, so that writers and artists who contribute to them are selling apples to people who already like apples. While a great number of newspapers in this country can certainly qualify as reactionary, I think the bulk of them are guilty of nothing worse than the ordinary mild conservatism that comes from the fact that it takes a man with money to own a newspaper these days.

Most papers are simply in the business to make money, just as the syndicates are. While they might object to a writer or an artist with a generally leftish trend, they are more than willing to put those objections aside if the feature rings the cash register downstairs in the business office by pulling in more readers, and consequently more advertisers at higher rates. There is no bar up to leftish contributors any more than there is one against extremely right-wing ones—all they have to do is to delight a high percentage of readers. No matter how much the harried editor is subjected to wails and threats by local pressure groups of business people, labor people, church people, or others, he is willing to put up with it if the feature that arouses their ire is a business asset. That is, unless his paper is one of the minority with such powerfully

"Of course, you mustn't misunderstand us — we all want a free press!"

strong editorial convictions that it won't run a rebellious feature under any circumstances. There are few of those. Even the Hearst papers, which have always set a high — or low — level of hysterical prejudice in the newspaper business, all publish Walter Winchell, whose views are generally so opposed to those of Hearst that his column has been referred to by its fans as the handy antidote that comes in the same package with the poison. Winchell's column is easily the biggest single asset to Hearst circulation.

Some of the worst newspapers in the country have the biggest circulation because they carry popular comic strips and features, so it hardly stands to reason that a feature creator doesn't have a chance for circulation if his politics are leftish. All he has to do is be popular with his readers, and almost anybody will print him, no matter how much they may gag while doing it. Of course, the complaining lefties do have this fact on their side of the argument: Because the general trend of newspaper

"Read all about it! Best comic strips in town! Read all about it!"

opinion in America is right wing, a mediocre feature can sell fairly well (just look at 'em) if its tone follows orthodox trends, while if a leftie seeks circulation, he must be doubly good. But to hell with that — a man with a mediocre offering has no right to complain anyway. The lefties who complain about the scarcity of newspapers with sincere editorial policies that are independent of influence from the business office should be thankful instead. If all papers, instead of trying to make money, took a high and mighty attitude and devoted themselves to making over the world in the image of their publishers, there would be no chance at all for anybody with radical ideas to get his stuff printed. As it is, us subversives can always find a way to sneak something into print, so long as we tickle somebody's funny bone or soothe him in his trouble, and he buys an extra paper.

The St. Louis *Post-Dispatch* cancellation was one of two very lucky things that happened to me early in 1946. The *Post-Dispatch* made me realize that while I was stumbling around in a fog of confusion and defiance about the syndicate's butchery of my drawings and the reaction of some newspapers around the country, I was turning out the kind of stuff that was costing me a lot of real friends who didn't object to my political views and who liked my social stuff but couldn't afford to devote space to printing the drawings when they completely lacked humor and perspective.

The second lucky thing was when the New York *Herald Tribune* started using my drawings after the New York *World-Telegram* threw them out because, as Roy Howard, the publisher, told me, I seemed to be following the Communist party line. The *Herald Tribune* is one of the most dignified, reputable, and generally conservative old newspapers in America. I like it because it confines its editorial opinions to the editorial page. Most papers that lean to the left or right have a way of playing up news stories that please them and playing down or altogether omitting those that cast some doubt on the validity of the editorial page.

The Republican *Herald Tribune* printed every single drawing I did from then on, putting them on the front page of the popular feature section, without a change in picture or caption, although some of the cartoons, such as the next one, were directly opposed to a column printed on the same page, or to an editorial a few pages away. That is liberal enough for me, thank you.

I guess everybody needs a knock to his ego once in a while, and the *Post-Dispatch* had provided that. But he needs a little confidence sometimes too, and the fact that the reputable *Herald Tribune* was willing to take a chance on my stuff, which was terrible at the time, in the hope that I would improve it, made me feel very fine. I like newspaper work, and the worst aspect of syndicates is that they are like big wholesale stores — your stuff is a product, merchandised and sold like soap, with an eye to pleasing the greatest number of customers most of the time. You don't feel that you're creating, but that you are manufacturing. That's why so many syndicated cartoonists end up by hiring a staff of assistants, including one to write the continuity, one to letter the words in the balloons, one to ink the drawings, and one to fill in backgrounds, so that the result contains very little work by the man who signs his name to it. I don't blame

"Sure it's a black-market price, lady—but don't your conscience feel better now that it's legal?"

the guys who do that. The syndicates demand a prodigious amount of production, which in itself is enough to keep a man from being very selective about the ideas or drawings he uses, and prevents him from throwing away stuff he is not satisfied with. And they don't give a damn how corny or terrible he is, just so he satisfies a lot of customers. Any man who goes into the business full of creative zeal and high ambitions is very lucky if he is able to hang onto those ideals, even though he does make a lot of money.

And the saddest thing of all is that the syndicates have fixed things so that cartoonists and writers and artists are practically forced to become syndicated before they can make a living. No matter how fine a job a man may do, or how much of a craftsman he may try to be, very few newspapers in America will hire him, because they can find something almost as good offered by a syndicate that sells the stuff to hundreds of other papers, and so is able to do it at a twentieth of the price. It's pretty awful to think of the thousands of talented characters in towns around the country who could have produced delightful local stuff which would have given the town paper real zest and personality, but who couldn't compete, even at starvation wages, with standardized and gutless comic strips and columns created thousands of miles away and offered dirt cheap to all comers.

These talents are forced to trot to New York or Chicago, where they might just possibly — the chances are slim — land themselves on a syndicate. There they are hacked and hammered and sawed until all their original appeal is gone, and they are pouring their stuff through a mold which has been found by long experience mildly to please most of the customers and to offend none of them.

I felt so bitter about syndicates by the time the *Herald Tribune* bought my stuff that when Helen Reid, the publisher, told me the Trib would hire me if I could get out of the syndicate, I jumped at the chance. The syndicate had been losing circulation so fast on my stuff that I thought they would be happy to release a feature that promised to become more of a liability than an asset. But the syndicate refused to release me, so I did the next best thing — I started hanging around the Trib where I could at least get the feeling I was doing individual work on an individual publication, and not trying to please every blasted editor and every blasted opinion in America.

"*Red, pink, left of center, colorless, careful, conservative, or reactionary?*"

Strangely enough, I stopped losing papers by leaps and bounds almost immediately. A few kept dribbling off for one reason or another, but almost half the number I had had at my peak were still buying the stuff. I didn't change my politics or my views, but I used a little more finesse in handling my political cartoons. And I found that I was beginning to learn enough about civilian life to provide me with some workable material, so I started branching out in my subject matter.

The prediction I had made to George Carlin a long time before had actually come true. The editors who still used my drawings totaled seventy-nine—the exact number that had reprinted my overseas stuff from *Stars and Stripes*, and who had used it because they thought it had some merit. The papers which had suddenly bought it for its curiosity value when *Time* had welcomed me home with a front cover and a most flattering and lengthy story inside, and the army had flown me as a VIP, were the ones who had dropped it like a hot potato, after complaining that they paid money for one thing and received something else.

Of course, this present seventy-nine wasn't exactly the same seventy-nine I had had two years before. Some of the old ones had dropped off, and some new ones had come in. But the list contained substantially the same names. In looking back over my personal postwar career, I'm amazed that I hung onto so many papers. For a while my stuff was so bad that it wouldn't have qualified for space in a mimeographed high-school paper. The editors who kept giving me space and paying me money during that time either didn't care what went into their papers, or they were mountains of patience who felt that I would have something better to offer when I got my personal life and my working problems straightened out. I like to think it was the latter, and I'm very grateful to them.

CHAPTER XIV

Like a lot of other people, I felt very warmly toward the Soviet Union right after the war. They had done a huge job and had suffered terribly in the fighting. We had in the past joined other great powers who had given the struggling Russian government the most hostile kind of treatment, and it seemed to me we should try to make up for it.

I felt guilty that my country had been one of those that had done so much to give Hitler aid and support while he was Nazifying Europe and building up a monstrous war machine — all for the purpose of building a "buffer" against Russia. I was bursting with so many sweet thoughts that I was willing to overlook the belligerent attitude Russia took toward us at the end of the war. After all, we had started the enmity, hadn't we? Nobody could blame Russia for being suspicious of the people who had been against her in the past, even though they had later fought on her side and enabled her to survive.

I wonder sometimes if the high-muck-a-mucks in the Kremlin are aware of the tremendous store of good will toward Russia there was in this country then. Despite the violent anti-Russian propaganda which had never ceased pouring from so many prominent newspapers and individuals, it's pretty safe to say that the majority opinion here was for leaning over backward to be friendly

"On second thought, I'd better receive Mr. Molotov in the drawing room."

with the Soviet. Perhaps the Kremlin made the mistake so many people abroad make, and thought that a sampling of the press in America and a daily perusal of political columns gave a reliable indication of public opinion. It is hard to believe that they could have been so misled. An overwhelming majority of American newspapers were anti-Roosevelt, yet Roosevelt was elected four times — to give only one of many examples proving that wherever the U. S. press goes, the nation generally goes elsewhere.

When the Kremlin sent Ilya Ehrenberg, one of its ace pretty-boys, to poke around in America after the war, he was swamped with admirers. I attended a party once where he gave a lecture and spouted the most tiresome line of guff about democracy, fascism, and progress you could ever hope to hear. The audience was not at all communist-inclined, but it gave him a terrific hand and a most sympathetic ear. It didn't particularly warm to him personally, but it was so anxious to be nice to Russia and her envoys that it did its best to give him a good impression to take home with him. I understand he went back to Russia and wrote a lot about the lynchings in the South. But he couldn't have helped telling his superiors how much everybody wanted to get along with Russia, and what with all the other observers they sent over here, they must have known a lot of us were willing to swallow almost anything to be nice to them.

But that reserve of good will is just about used up. My sugary feelings toward Russia disappeared when their behavior in the UN became as boorish as their activities outside it. I don't pretend to know all their reasons and tactics, but I do know their official excuse for their

285

"Cable that idiot at UN and ask him whether he's working for us or the rest of the damn world."

actions at UN. They claim that none of the other great powers entered the United Nations in good faith, or for any other reason besides self-interest. They claim that England and America are spending every waking moment trying to figure out ways to encircle, contain, and destroy

286

them and their way of life. They claim they are forced to look out for themselves.

I can pretty well agree with all but the last. It is painfully obvious that England's high brass fought two wars between 1939 and 1945 — one to whip the Germans immediately and the other to louse up Russia in the future. To find out what some Americans would like to do to Russia, just pick up a newspaper and read it. Certainly if the Churchills and the Hoovers had the run of their respective countries, Russia would be justified in taking almost any drastic step for self-protection, including the misuse of her powers in the United Nations.

Experts recommend use of food as best political weapon in Europe. **News Item**

But the Churchills and the Hoovers don't have the run of their countries. It is still the people marking ballots who have the say-so, and after the war those people were almost unanimously clamoring for a successful United Nations and an end to international feuding. If Russia

"I got a conscience I can't make just anybody th' people's choice."

"Hiyah, cannon fodder."

had shown any eagerness to make UN work or had displayed anything but cynicism and self-interest, the people in England and America would have forced their leaders to follow suit. Instead, Russia's behavior has given professional red-baiters all over the world a chance to say almost anything they please and get away with it. It has given the Churchill and Hoover factions a plausible reason for selling the idea of preparing for another war.

I'm sore at Russia because she has enabled all the little Hitler-lovers and Franco-lovers and Perón-lovers and 200 per cent pure-blooded nationalistic-white-gentile-Protestant Americans of the Gerald Smith variety to come out of their stinking holes in the floor. They represent themselves as saviors of the world and find sympathetic listeners only two short years after we finished fighting a war against their kind. I'm hopping mad at the glorious Soviet Union because if she had behaved, the Dies-Rankin-Thomas Un-American Activities Gestapo would

"They may not smell good, but they say they hate communism."

have been laughed right out of Congress, and the assorted little mice would have stayed in their holes, knowing they would be booed off any lecture platform in the country.

Adolf Hitler, who is now in a position to relax and enjoy things, must be splitting with laughter as he fans himself with a morning newspaper in the intense heat of his residence and reads about the state of the world today.

"My *patient!*"

The leftists who formed the backbone of resistance in Axis-occupied countries during the war are now classified by us as guerrillas, murderers, and renegades. The extreme right-wing regimes, which sympathized and actually collaborated with the Axis in many cases, are getting guns and money and support from us in their campaign to wipe out the "renegades," who are often far more representative of their people. We are doing this to protect ourselves from Russia, who in turn is not above any kind of trickery to protect herself from us.

The magnificent Allies are making magnificent asses of themselves, which ought to be enough to make Adolf gleeful, but he must be prostrated with happiness over what is happening in Germany. The grand old Reich is now on the road to rapid recovery. The old girl has several very influential doctors eager to put her back on her feet. Englishmen, Russians, and Americans are being told by their respective leaders that a happy and prosperous Germany is essential to a happy and prosperous Europe. Already Americans and Englishmen are planning a way to use Germany as a buffer against Russia, and Russia is working hard to convince the Germans that she would make a fine buffer against England and America. Hitler did his work well.

"It's Hoover's report on Germany. I'll read it if ya promise to muffle yer sobs."

My feeling about the behavior of the Allies at the end of the war has made me do some pretty pessimistic cartoons about the United Nations. This has caused me some trouble with people who tell me not to be cynical about it because if nobody believes in UN it will never work. I think there is a hell of a difference between cynicism and pessimism. A person who is cynical about the idea of a UN thinks that human nature and selfishness will always cause war and that anything designed to

"I just had a sudden thought. Them delegates might start behavin' themselves if we refuse to build 'em an air-raid shelter."

prevent armed conflicts is a waste of time. A pessimist merely thinks UN is doomed to failure unless something happens to change the way it's going. And I believe it's silly to gloss over that fact, shut both eyes, repeat "UN will work" fifty times a night, and maybe do a little knee-bending on a prayer rug.

"We seem to be the only survivors. Let's unite."

"Good heavens! I'd swear I heard one of the pieces groan!"

Considering all the things that have been done to sabotage UN, it is a little amazing that it is still functioning, and is even optimistic enough to start work on a group of fancy buildings in New York. The saboteurs are the nationalists all over the world who fought the League of Nations to the death and learned a few tricks while doing it. The American saboteurs think any system of world co-operation that includes the United States means that George Spelvin, the poor bastard, might have to use the same car for five years. The British saboteurs think — and probably correctly — that the Empire will have an awful time if UN starts investigating some of its colonies and possessions and the conditions of the people in them. The Russian saboteurs know blasted well that if UN is successful and is able to send investigators around to keep nations from preparing for war and getting into trouble, their precious sovereignty will be pierced. The big powers, without which the UN can't possibly exist, are carrying on their old chess game all over the globe.

It will be curious to see, if enough of us survive to compile objective history books, just which nation of the big three has been most responsible for the failings of the United Nations. Anybody who is willing to guess is either extremely brilliant or extremely prejudiced. I find it very easy to blame Russia because the Russians have been far less subtle in their sabotaging than anybody else, but I'm far from sure.

In the middle of 1947 I received a telegram signed by former Supreme Court Justice Owen J. Roberts, which had been sent to a number of people around the country. It read:

"AM DEEPLY CONCERNED ABOUT POSSIBILITY OF CONGRESS NOT TAKING PROMPT ACTION ON UNIVERSAL MILITARY TRAINING FOLLOWING PUBLICATION OF COMPTON REPORT WHICH ADVANCES COMPELLING REASONS FOR IMMEDIATE ADOPTION. MEASURE CAN PASS THIS SESSION IF LEADING

Flattered that I should receive a communiqué from such a distinguished gentleman, and doubly flattered that a person of my tender age and questionable politics should be referred to as a leading citizen, I said yes by return wire.

When the CECUMT letterhead (see wire for explanation of initials) came out with my name on it, it was like old times for a while. *Time,* which had ignored me for a long lonely period after I had betrayed its earlier confidence in me by becoming a "fellow traveler," sent a couple of nice people around to interview me. Then it ran a full-column story called "Education of a G.I.," telling how I had learned a bitter lesson which all youngsters who fellow-travel must learn. By a strange coincidence, the cartoon about a couple of Russian jail-keepers came out about the same time as the CECUMT circular, and *Time* ran it as the centerpiece of the story. Actually, I had done a number of anti-Russian cartoons before that, but *Time* people are busy people and they couldn't be blamed for not reading my trenchant stuff *every* day.

After the *Time* piece appeared, the syndicate got cheerful about me, and I was told I might even get back some canceled contracts from newspapers that had dropped me in my radical days. I honestly believe that for a couple of weeks there I could have sold a high-priced magazine article telling all about my conversion (political).

My reason for saying yes to Justice Roberts was simply

"General, I want you to find out why the army isn't getting more recruits."

that I am no longer sure that the UN can be depended upon to keep the peace. I don't belong in the ranks of those who say a war between Russia and the West is inevitable, but I certainly believe it is a growing possibility. I would much rather see the UN have the only army, navy, and air force in the world, plus control of the atomic bomb and other superweapons. But evidently such ideas will be vigorously opposed by all the big peace-loving nations as a threat to their idea of peace. A stuffy UN investigator might poke around and turn up a poison-gas or machine-gun factory, thereby violating somebody's precious peace-loving sovereignty. So long as UN is kept ineffectual by its members, so long as the world respects only force, I want my country to be strong enough to take care of itself.

"I've already planned his school, college, branch of service, and veterans' organization."

"I do hope I won't be disillusioned."

I have heard people say we should be strong so that if there is another war we can win it, then show the world the right way to live afterward. This is old stuff, and it is poppycock. Our behavior hardly qualifies us as world leaders. Ours is one of the most conservative governments in the world today, and one of the most bumbling. We have more provincialism and bigotry and superstition and prejudice per square mile than almost any other nation. We like to think of ourselves as a young, progressive country, but, while we do have energy, we have become smug and self-satisfied.

We do have one thing — a fairly free opportunity to say what we think. Despite the Dies Committee, Harry Truman's "loyalty tests," and the fact that people do lose jobs for having the "wrong" politics, it is still possible to join political movements and express opinions without too much fear of going to jail. I think this is one thing that gives this country the right to survive. The people in it like to think for themselves and to be individuals, and anybody is going to have a hard time talking them out of it.

I don't want to see Russia win if there is another war, because that country has proved it is capable only of replacing one kind of tyranny with another. I want my bumbling side to win, because where there is a chance for free speech and honest thinking there is always hope that something decent will eventually come out of the chaos which would result from that war. I hope it doesn't ever come to that, but so long as the UN is hamstrung by the selfish interests of its members, I feel pretty grim about the future.

If we must become strong in arms again, we should agitate against the professional militarists, the imperialists, the bigots, and the little Führers in our midst; it would be a terrible thing if the strength we built up fell into their hands. And we have even more reason to raise hell about our policy of buddying up with the world's worst characters — many of whom were recently our enemies —

"I'd swear he licked his chops as we went by."

and lending support to oppressive regimes such as those in Greece and China. I think our way of life can bear inspection if it needs the world's fascists for allies.

One of my pet cartoon subjects in recent months has been military versus civilian control of atomic energy.

So long as we have that damn bomb, I think it is one of the most important controversies in the world. If the pro-military side wins, my pessimism about the future is going to turn into real despair. I've done a lot of drawings about it because I think most military people are

"*Poppa is only a scientist, Junior. The* smart *men decide how to use my inventions.*"

destructive by training and by necessity and would take this force and use it to wreck everything. They would unquestionably succeed in making the United States lord and master of the globe. This would cause a lot of people to go to the trouble of bringing about a revolution to unseat us, because we would behave exactly like every

"I didn't raise my boy to be a soldier. . . ."

other lord and master of the earth. I would rather see the thing in the hands of civilians with milder ambitions.

It has been revealing to watch the positions taken by various statesmen and prominent people in this controversy. Those who look upon the atom as a simple solution to our world problems and as an obvious answer

to the Red Menace are agitating to place it in the hands
of the military, and their excuse is ludicrous. They say
it would be safer with the tight-lipped army than with

*"Just leave it to us, old man. Look what we did for the
Wright brothers. . . ."*

TEQUILA, N.M.
POPULATION 79
NOT COUNTING
210 POETS
97 ARTISTS
18 NUCLEAR
   PHYSICISTS
7 F.B.I. AGENTS
3 COLONELS
1 GENERAL

NEW MEXICO

the scientists who invented it, many of whom are thinking persons, and might even be radical.

I spent the summer of 1946 in Santa Fe, New Mexico, near Los Alamos. I was also in the southern part of the state, a few miles from the White Sands experimental grounds where they were popping off V-2's and other assorted superfirecrackers. Consequently, I had the opportunity of sitting around in restaurants and bars where the soldiers, officers, and scientists came in for refreshment and sociable company. Any resident of the area will tell you that it is a fairly easy thing to get a soldier or an officer to talk about his job, but the scientists seem to have a fearful reticence about anything connected with physics, or the state of the weather, or anything else that might be interpreted as scientific data.

Since the army people in those projects are used for routine duties and seldom have more than a nodding acquaintance with the ultrasecret mechanisms, they haven't much information to give, but many of them are eager to impress any audience with the importance of their jobs. I remember an army captain in the café of La Fonda in Santa Fe, who was loudly telling the people at his table that he had been privileged to see the first bomb set off, and he undertook to describe to them the size of the

"One more stupid mistake and I'll transfer you to a desk job on the atomic bomb commission!"

"To hell with its food value—will it explode?"

thing. They were civilians and they were naturally goggle-eyed at the prospect of hearing secret stuff, even though the captain's eagerness to talk made it doubtful that he had seen very much. I know the army pretty well, and I know that the more a superior officer tries to impress his underlings with the importance of silence, the more gossipy they get. To turn the atom loose in the land of latrine rumor would be disastrous.

Sometimes I really wonder why anybody thought to ask me to come out in favor of universal military training. I don't trust the army, I don't like the army, and I even poke fun at its recruiting program. Perhaps, under all

"Cheer up, gents. If worst comes to worst, at least our families will be here with us."

the pompous and high-sounding words I have mouthed about why we should have an army, I want it around so I can draw more pictures about it.

It's very tough to live in this country and cling **to**

young ideals. Some people have been able to do it, but they are rare, and any of us who thinks he can do it before he tries it is guilty of considerable smugness. Every day I grow older I find it easier to adjust myself to our society; every day Europe and its people, as I saw them, grow more remote to me.

I am even getting used to the Throckmortons who love the smell of gunpowder and who explain why it is to our advantage to use the atomic bomb while we have it. I have become so tolerant that I forget to remind them

"*. . . an' my conclusion is that wars is impossible unless both sides is right.*"

"I say it's war, Throckmorton, and I say let's fight!"

it would be nice if they consulted the young men who will have to do the dirty work if an atomic war comes about. It is a sure sign that I am getting a little older and more mature.

I look back at the cartoon of the kid explaining about war in his classroom, and I think what a silly thing that was for me to draw. What business do little squeakers have talking such fancy talk? I look at the drawing of the Russian soldier and the American soldier drinking together, and I remember what I had in mind when I drew it. I figured that the soldiers and the farmers and

"I hear Moscow an' Washington are snappin' at each other again, Ivan."

the clerks, with their wives, kids, and dependents, have a way of getting along with each other all over the world and have a common interest that keeps them from being natural enemies. They all want a little health, a decent job, a comfortable family, and a reasonable amount of security. I remember how German prisoners, Italian prisoners, French soldiers, British soldiers, American soldiers, soldiers from almost every nation whether they were officially enemies or friends, had a way of exchanging snapshots of each other's families and discussing such popular subjects as automobiles and liquor.

Now I don't find myself thinking so much about that. I have been living long enough in this country which is so isolated from the facts of life, to find it easy to think of Russia or France or Italy in terms of nations and politics, not as groups of millions of individuals who want the same things I do.

Every once in a while I rebel against the Throckmortons and turn out a picture about the Republican Congress, which has distinguished itself by jumping backward over a span of almost twenty years and putting us where we were before the depression of 1929. But I find myself doing less and less of that stuff and more and more little pictures of life in America — kids, cops, and dogs.

I'm sure I'll continue drawing about politics once in a while, but I got my big burden off my chest by getting this book out. I don't ask anybody to agree with me, nor do I hope to convince any readers of anything. I simply feel age creeping up; my bank account grows, my radical years are almost over. I want to stick this thing on my bookshelf as a reminder of my wild days so

I can read it over and be a little more tolerant of the next generation of upstarts.

"Zat's just like parents. Zey always leave their messes for their kids to clean up."